D0908095

A Guide To

The Hidden Wisdom
of Kabbalah

The Hidden Wisdom
of Kabbalah

With Ten Complete Kabbalah Lessons

BY

RABBI MICHAEL LAITMAN

COMPILED BY BENZION GIERTZ

LAITMAN
Kabbalah
Publishers

Executive Editor: Benzion Giertz

Laitman Kabbalah Publishers Website:
www.kabbalah.info
Laitman Kabbalah Publishers Email:
info@kabbalah.info

ISBN: ISBN: 0-973190914
Second Edition: November 2003

*W*hile it is great and worthwhile publicizing that there is an incomparably wonderful quality to studying Kabbalah wisdom, even though they do not know what they are studying, it is the tremendous desire to understand what they are studying that awakens the lights surrounding their soul.

Rabbi Yehuda Ashlag
"Introduction to the Study of the Ten Sefirot"

Kabbalists throughout the generations referred to our time as the turning point, after which mass apprehension of the spiritual realm would begin. Kabbalah is gaining popularity, despite the fact that very few people really understand what it is about, why it is called a secret science, how people come to it, etc. However, the eagerness is already felt among the masses, exactly as the great Kabbalists prophesized many centuries ago.

Rabbi Michael Laitman

About the Book

The Kabbalist Rabbi Laitman, who was the student and personal assistant to Rabbi Baruch Ashlag from 1979-1991, follows in the footsteps of his rabbi in passing on the wisdom of Kabbalah to the world. This book is based on sources that were passed down by Rabbi Baruch's father, Rabbi Yehuda Ashlag (Baal HaSulam), the author of "the Sulam," the commentaries on The Book of Zohar, who continued the ways of the Ari and Rabbi Shimon Bar Yochai and many great Kabbalists throughout the generations before them. A unique method of study that was also passed down in the same manner provides individuals with precise tools and an appropriate atmosphere for embarking on a highly efficient path of self-discovery and spiritual ascent. The focus of these studies is primarily on initiating profound inner processes that individuals undergo at their own pace, with no regard to race, age, gender, marital status or religious affiliation.

With the goal of this book being to assist individuals in confronting the first stages of the spiritual realm, we have included ten complete Kabbalah lessons that can be used for spreading this wisdom to anyone seeking practical guidance to understanding the world we live in. This unique method of study, which encourages sharing this wisdom with others, not only helps overcome the trials and tribulations of everyday life, but initiates a process in which individuals extend themselves beyond the standard limitations of today's world.

Benzion Giertz
Executive Editor

Contents

Part I
The Need for Kabbalah in Our Daily Lives

Part II
Ten Kabbalah Lessons

Introduction

The laws of nature, our place in the world and our behavior have been studied by scientists and philosophers for thousands of years.

Along with logical assumptions, science uses quantifiable research and data. Yet our scientists and researchers have discovered that the more they advance in their research, the more obscure and confusing they find the world to be.

Science has undoubtedly brought enormous progress into the world, yet it is limited. Scientific tools cannot measure man's inner world, his soul, behavior and sources of motivation. Man, the major component of the creation, is still left without knowledge about his role in this universe.

Man has always looked for answers to the basic questions of life: Who am I? What is the purpose of my being here? Why does the world exist? Do we continue to exist after our physical being has completed its tasks?

In this world of constant pressure, some find temporary satisfaction in Eastern techniques, measures aimed at relaxation, or reducing suffering by minimizing personal expectations and desires. Various forms of meditation, nutrition, and physical and mental exercise quiet man's natural instincts and enable him to feel more comfortable from the point of view of his physical state. This process teaches him to lower his expectations, yet leaves him in conflict with his true desires.

Our life experience teaches us that we have unlimited desires— and only limited resources to satisfy them. This is the primary reason there is no way to completely satisfy all our desires and therefore avoid suffering. That is the subject of Kabbalah. Kabbalah answers the basic questions of life and guides us toward achieving unlimited satisfaction on a daily basis.

The essential questions of man's being add another dimension to human suffering. They do not allow us to feel satisfied even when this or that goal has been fulfilled. When one attains the goal he strives for, he immediately feels he's missing yet another pleasure. This prevents him from enjoying his achievements, and his suffering is renewed. In retrospect, he sees that he has spent most of his time making an effort to achieve his goals, and has gained very little pleasure from the successes themselves.

Everyone, each in his own way, tries to answer these questions from the sources of information at his disposal. Each one of us formulates our own perception of the world based on our experience. Reality and everyday life constantly put this perception to the test, making us react, improve, or otherwise change it. With some of us, this process occurs on a conscious level; with others it happens unconsciously.

Kabbalah reaches out to all those who are seeking awareness. It teaches you how to add an essential feeling of the spiritual sphere—the sixth sense—that will affect your life in this world. This will allow you to perceive the upper world—the Creator—and to gain control over your life.

The Bible, The Zohar, The Tree of Life and other authentic spiritual sources were set down in order to teach us how to progress in the spiritual realms, to study them and to receive spiritual knowledge. They explain how to set out on a path to spiritual ascent in this world. Over the generations, Kabbalists have written many books in various styles, each in accordance with the era in which they lived.

In total, four languages were created to introduce us to our spiritual reality: the language of the Bible (which includes the Five Books of Moses, the Prophets and the Scriptures), the language of legends, a legalistic language, and the language of Kabbalah, which describes the spiritual upper-worlds system and how to reach it. The differences in languages simply present various perspectives on the same subject in different formats—each suiting the generation it was intended for.

The Kabbalist Baal HaSulam writes in his book Fruits of the Wise:

> The inner wisdom of Kabbalah is the same as that of the Bible, The Zohar and the legends, with the only difference between them being the manner of the logic. It is rather like an ancient tongue translated into four languages. It is self-evident that the wisdom itself did not change at all due to the change in language. All we need to consider is which is most convenient and widely accepted for conveyance.

By reading this book, you will be able to take your first steps in understanding the roots of human behavior and the laws of nature. The contents present the essential principles of the Kabbalistic approach and describe the wisdom of Kabbalah and the way it works. *A Guide to the Hidden Wisdom of Kabbalah* is intended for those searching for a sensible and reliable method of studying the phenomena of our world, for those seeking to understand the reasons for suffering and pleasure, for those seeking answers to the major questions of life.

Part I

The Need for Kabbalah in Our Daily Lives

Chapter 1

What is Kabbalah?

Kabbalah is an accurate method to investigate and define man's position in the universe. The wisdom of Kabbalah tells us the reason why man exists, why he is born, why he lives, what the purpose of his life is, where he comes from and where he is going after he completes his life in this world.

Kabbalah is a method of reaching the spiritual world. It teaches us about the spiritual world, and by studying it, we develop another sense. With the help of this sense we can be in touch with the upper worlds.

Kabbalah is not a theoretical study, but a very practical one. Man learns about himself, who he is, what he is like. He learns what he needs to do to change himself stage by stage and step by step. He conducts his research through his inner self.

All experimentation is conducted on himself, within himself. That is why Kabbalah is called "The Hidden Wisdom." Through Kabbalah a person undergoes internal changes that only he feels and knows are taking place. This activity occurs within a person; it is unique to him, and only he knows about it.

The word Kabbalah comes from the Hebrew word *lekabbel*, to receive. Kabbalah describes the motives of actions as "the desire to receive." This desire refers to receiving various kinds of pleasure. In order to receive pleasure, a person is usually willing to invest great effort.

The question is, how can one attain the maximum amount of pleasure while paying a minimum price for it? Everyone tries to answer this question in his own way.

There is a certain order to the way the desire to receive develops and grows. In the first stage, man lusts after physical pleasure. Then he seeks money and honor. An even stronger desire makes him thirst for power. He may later develop a desire for spirituality, which is at the peak of the pyramid. A person who recognizes how great his desire for spirituality begins to seek ways of satisfying this desire.

The passage through the stages of the desire to receive makes a person become familiar with his abilities and limitations.

Kabbalah deals with the upper worlds, the roots of our feelings and thoughts, which we cannot grasp. Since we have no control over the worlds, we do not know how and why our feelings and thoughts are created. We wonder at experiences such as sweet, bitter, pleasant, rough and so forth. We are unsuccessful at building scientific tools to examine our feelings, even in the field of psychology, psychiatry and other social disciplines. Behavioral factors remain hidden from our understanding.

Kabbalah is a system for scientifically evaluating our feelings: It takes the total of our feelings and desires, and provides an exact scientific formula for each and every phenomenon, at each level, for every type of understanding and feeling.

This is the work of feelings combined with intellect. It uses, for beginning students, geometry, matrices and diagrams. When studying Kabbalah, they recognize each of their own feelings and begin to understand it. They know what name it should be given according to its power, direction and character.

The wisdom of Kabbalah is an ancient and proven method. Through it, man can receive higher awareness and attain spirituality. This is really his goal in this world. When a person feels a desire for spirituality, he starts to feel a longing for it, and can then develop the desire through the wisdom of Kabbalah that has been provided by the Creator.

Kabbalah is a word that describes the aim of the Kabbalist: to attain everything man is capable of, as a thinking being, the highest of all creatures.

Chapter 2

Why Study Kabbalah?

When an ordinary person studies the writings of the Kabbalists, he learns about what was formerly hidden from him. Only after acquiring the sixth sense through study does he begin to feel and see what was previously unrevealed.

Everyone has a natural ability to develop this sixth sense, and that is the reason Kabbalists transmit their knowledge of the structure of the upper, spiritual world. [See the chapter on "Sensing Reality through Kabbalah."]

When a person is exposed to Kabbalistic materials, he may not at first grasp what he is reading. But if he wants to understand, and tries to do so in the proper manner, he invokes what is called the Surrounding Light, the light that corrects him; and very gradually he is shown his spiritual reality. The terms "to correct" and "correction" are used in Kabbalah to describe a change in the desire to receive, i.e., to acquire the qualities of the spiritual world and of the Creator.

Everyone has this sixth, still-dormant spiritual sense; this is called the point of the heart. Opposite it stands the light, which will eventually fill the point, the sixth sense, when it develops.

The sixth sense is also called the spiritual Vessel (*Kli*), and it continues to exist even without material reality. The spiritual Vessel of the ordinary person who has never studied Kabbalah is not sufficiently developed to feel the spiritual world. When he studies the original Kabbalah writings in the proper way, this light enlightens the point of the heart and begins to develop it. The point then begins to widen and it expands sufficiently to allow the Surrounding Light to enter it. When the light enters into the point of the heart, it gives a person a spiritual feeling. This point is the person's soul.

Nothing is possible without help from the upper world, without the Surrounding Light descending from above and gradually lighting the way for a person. Even when we do not recognize this light, there is a direct connection between the point of the heart and the light due to fill it, as planned from above. Studying Kabbalah books enables a person to connect to the source of the light, and gradually come to feel a desire for spirituality. This process is called *segula* (remedy).

Rabbi Yehuda Ashlag wrote in the Introduction to the Study of the Ten Sefirot:

> Accordingly, why did the Kabbalists instruct everyone to study Kabbalah? While it is great and worthwhile publicizing that there is an incomparably wonderful quality to studying Kabbalah wisdom, even though they do not know what they are studying, it is the tremendous desire to understand what they are studying that awakens the lights surrounding their soul. That means that every person is assured the possibility of eventually attaining all the wonderful achievements the Creator intended for us in planning Creation.
>
> Those who do not attain them in this incarnation will do so in another, until the Creator's intention is fulfilled. Even if a person does not achieve this completion, the lights are destined to be his; the Surrounding Lights wait for him to prepare his Vessel to receive them. Therefore, even when he lacks the Vessels, when a person is engaged in this wisdom and recalls the names of the lights and Vessels waiting and belonging to him, they will shine on him but only to a certain degree. But they will not penetrate his inner soul, since his Vessels are not yet

ready to accept them. Kabbalah is the only means to create the Vessel to receive the light of the Creator. The light he receives when he is engaged in the wisdom imparts to him a grace from above, bestowing an abundance of holiness and purity on him, bringing him closer to reaching completion.

Kabbalah is special in that it gives a person a taste of spirituality while he is studying, and from that experience he comes to prefer spirituality to materialism. In proportion to his spirituality, he clarifies his will and learns to distance himself from things he was once attracted to, much as an adult is no longer attracted to childish games.

Why do we need Kabbalah? Because Kabbalah is given to us as a springboard for change. It is given to us so that we can know and perceive the Creator at any given moment throughout the day. These are the only reasons why the wisdom of Kabbalah was provided. Whoever learns Kabbalah in order to alter himself and improve himself, in order to know the Creator, reaches the stage in which he begins to see he can improve, and fulfill his true destiny in this lifetime.

Chapter 3

Who is a Kabbalist?

The Kabbalist is a researcher who studies his nature using a proven, time-tested and accurate method. He studies the essence of his existence using tools we can all utilize—feelings, intellect and heart.

A Kabbalist looks like an ordinary person. He need not have any special skills, talents, or occupation. He need not be a wise man or wear a holy expression. At some point in his life, this ordinary person decided to look for a way in which he would find credible answers to the questions that were troubling him. By utilizing a distinct method of learning, he was successful in acquiring an extra sense—a sixth sense—which is the spiritual sense.

Through this sense, the Kabbalist feels the spiritual spheres as a clear reality, just as we feel our reality here; he receives knowledge about the spiritual spheres, the upper worlds, and the revelation of higher forces. These worlds are called upper worlds, since they are higher than and beyond our world.

The Kabbalist ascends from his current spiritual level to the next one. This movement brings him from one upper world to the next. He sees the roots from which everything that exists here has developed, everything that fills our world, including ourselves. The Kabbalist is simultaneously in our world, and in the upper worlds. This quality is shared by all Kabbalists.

Kabbalists receive the real information that surrounds us, and feel this reality. Therefore, they can study it, be familiar with it, and teach us about it. They provide a new method through which we can meet the source of our lives, leading us to spirituality. They use books that are written in a special language. We must read these books in a special way, so they become a Vessel for discovering the truth for us as well.

In the books they have written, the Kabbalists inform us about the techniques based on man's personal experiences. From their all-encompassing point of view, they have found the way to help those who would follow, and then climb the same ladder as they did. Their method is called the wisdom of Kabbalah.

Chapter 4

The History of Kabbalah and The Zohar

The first Kabbalist we know of was the patriarch Abraham. He saw the wonders of human existence, asked questions of the Creator, and the upper worlds were revealed to him. The knowledge he acquired, and the method used in its acquisition, he passed on to coming generations. Kabbalah was passed among the Kabbalists from mouth to mouth for many centuries. Each Kabbalist added his unique experience and personality to this body of accumulated knowledge. Their spiritual achievements were described in the language relevant to the souls of their generation.

Kabbalah continued to develop after the Bible (the Five Books of Moses) was written. In the period between the First and Second Temples (586 BCE — 515 BCE), it was already being studied in groups. Following the destruction of the Second Temple (70 CE) and until the current generation, there have been three particularly important periods in the development of Kabbalah, during which the most important writings on Kabbalah study methods were issued.

The first period occurred during the 2nd century, when the book of The Zohar was written by Rabbi Shimon Bar Yochai, "the Rashbi." This was around the year 150 CE. Rabbi Shimon was a pupil of the famous Rabbi Akiva (40 CE — 135 CE). Rabbi Akiva and several of his disciples were tortured and killed by the Romans, who felt threatened by his teaching of the Kabbalah. They flayed his skin and stripped his bones with an iron scraper (like today's currycomb) for cleaning their horses. Following the death of 24,000 of Rabbi Akiva's disciples, the Rashbi was authorized by Rabbi Akiva and Rabbi Yehuda Ben Baba to teach future generations the Kabbalah as it had been taught to him. Rabbi Shimon Bar Yochai and four others were the only ones to survive. Following the capture and imprisonment of Rabbi Akiva, the Rashbi escaped with his son, Elazar. They hid in a cave for 13 years.

They emerged from the cave with The Zohar, and with a crystallized method for studying Kabbalah and achieving spirituality. The Rashbi reached the 125 levels man can achieve during his life in this world. The Zohar tells us that he and his son reached the level called "Eliyahu the Prophet," meaning that the Prophet himself came to teach them.

The Zohar is written in a unique form; it is in the form of parables and is presented in Aramaic, a language spoken in biblical times. The Zohar tells us that Aramaic is "the reverse side of Hebrew," the hidden side of Hebrew. Rabbi Shimon Bar Yochai did not write this himself; he conveyed the wisdom and the way to reach it in an organized manner by dictating its contents to Rabbi Aba. Aba rewrote The Zohar in such a way that only those who are worthy of understanding would be able to do so.

The Zohar explains that human development is divided into 6,000 years, during which time souls undergo a continuous process of development in each generation. At the end of the process souls reach a position of "the end of correction," i.e., the highest level of spirituality and wholeness.

Rabbi Shimon Bar Yochai was one of the greatest of his generation. He wrote and interpreted many Kabbalistic subjects that were published and are well known to this day. On the other hand, the book of The Zohar, disappeared after it was written.

According to legend, The Zohar writings were kept hidden in a cave in the vicinity of Safed in Israel. They were found several hundred years later by Arabs residing in the area. A Kabbalist from Safed purchased some fish at the market one day, and was astonished to discover the priceless value of the paper in which they had been wrapped. He immediately set about purchasing the remaining pieces of paper from the Arabs, and collected them into a book.

This happened because the nature of hidden things is such that they must be discovered at a suitable moment, when suitable souls reincarnate and enter into our world. That is how The Zohar came to be revealed over time.

The study of these writings was conducted in secret by small groups of Kabbalists. The first publication of this book was by Rabbi Moshe de Leon, in the 13th century in Spain.

The second period of the development of Kabbalah is very important to the Kabbalah of our generation. This is the period of "the Ari," Rabbi Yitzhak Luria, who created the transition between the two methods of Kabbalah study. The first time the pure language of Kabbalah appeared was in the writings of the Ari. The Ari proclaimed the start of a period of open mass study of Kabbalah.

The Ari was born in Jerusalem in 1534. A child when his father died, his mother took him to Egypt where he grew up in his uncle's home.

During his life in Egypt, he made his living in commerce but devoted most of his time to studying Kabbalah. Legend has it that he spent seven years in isolation on the island of

Roda on the Nile where he studied The Zohar, books by the first Kabbalists, and writings by another rabbi of his generation, "the Ramak," Rabbi Moshe Cordovero.

In 1570, the Ari arrived in Safed, Israel. Despite his youth, he immediately started teaching Kabbalah. His greatness was soon recognized; all the wise men of Safed, who were very knowledgeable in the hidden and revealed Wisdom, came to study with him, and he became famous. For a year-and-a-half his disciple Rabbi Chaim Vital committed to paper the answers to many of the questions that arose during his studies.

The Ari left behind a basic system for studying Kabbalah, which is still in use today. Some of these writings are *Etz Hachayim* (The Tree of Life), *Sha'ar HaKavanot* (The Gateway of Intentions), *Sha'ar HaGilgulim* (The Gateway of Reincarnation), and others. The Ari died in 1572, still a young man. His writings were archived according to his last wish, in order not to reveal his doctrine before the time was ripe.

The great Kabbalists provided the method and taught it, but knew that their generation was still unable to appreciate its dynamics. Therefore, they often preferred to hide or even burn their writings. We know that Baal HaSulam burned and destroyed a major part of his writings. There is special significance in this fact that the knowledge was committed to paper, and later destroyed. Whatever is revealed in the material world affects the future, and is revealed easier the second time.

Rabbi Vital ordered other parts of the Ari's writings to be hidden and buried with him. A portion was handed down to his son, who arranged the famous writings, The Eight Gates. Much later, a group of scholars headed by Rabbi Vital's grandson removed another portion from the grave.

Study of The Zohar in groups started openly only during the period of the Ari. The study of The Zohar then prospered for two hundred years. In the great Hassidut period (1750 — to the end of the 19th century), almost every great rabbi was a Kabbalist. Kabbalists appeared, mainly in Poland, Russia, Morocco, Iraq, Yemen and several other countries. Then, at the beginning of the 20th century, interest in Kabbalah waned until it almost completely disappeared.

The third period of the development of Kabbalah contains an additional method to the Ari's doctrines, written in this generation by Rabbi Yehuda Ashlag, who authored the commentary of the *Sulam* (ladder) of The Zohar, and the Ari's teachings. His method is particularly suited to the souls of the current generation.

Rabbi Yehuda Ashlag is known as "Baal HaSulam" for his rendition of the Sulam of The Zohar. Born in 1885 in Lodz, Poland, he absorbed a deep knowledge of the written and oral law in his youth, and later became a judge and teacher in Warsaw. In 1921, he immigrated to Israel with his family and became the rabbi of Givat Shaul in Jerusalem. He was already immersed in writing his own doctrine when he began to pen the commentary of The Zohar in 1943. Baal HaSulam finished writing his commentary of The Zohar in 1953. He died the following year and was buried in Jerusalem at the Givat Shaul cemetery.

His eldest son, Rabbi Baruch Shalom Ashlag, "the Rabash," became his successor. His books are structured according to his father's instructions. They gracefully elaborate on his father's writings, facilitating our comprehension of his father's commentaries as handed down to our generation.

The Rabash was born in Warsaw in 1907 and immigrated to Israel with his father. Only after Rabbi Baruch was married did his father include him in study groups of selected students learning the hidden wisdom of Kabbalah. He was soon allowed to teach his father's new students.

Following his father's death, he took it upon himself to continue teaching the special method he had learned. Despite his great achievements, like his father, he insisted on keeping to a very modest way of life. During his lifetime he worked as a cobbler, construction worker and clerk. Externally, he lived like any ordinary person, but devoted every spare moment to studying and teaching Kabbalah. The Rabash died in 1991.

Rabbi Yehuda Ashlag, the Baal HaSulam, is the recognized spiritual leader for our generation. He is the only one in this generation who has written a fully comprehensive and updated commentary of The Zohar and the writings of the Ari. These books, with the addition of his son Rabbi Baruch Ashlag's essays, are the only source we can use to assist us in further progress.

When we study their books, we are actually studying The Zohar and the Ari's writings through the most recent commentaries (of the past 50 years). This is a life belt for our generation, since it enables us to study ancient texts as if they had been written now, and to use them as a springboard to spirituality.

Baal HaSulam's method suits everyone, and the *sulam* (ladder) he built in his writings ensures that none of us need fear studying Kabbalah. Anyone learning Kabbalah is assured that within three to five years he will be able to reach spiritual spheres, all realities and divine understanding, which is the name given to that which is above and beyond us and not yet felt by us. If we study according to the books of Rabbi Yehuda Ashlag, the Baal HaSulam, we can reach true correction.

The study method is constructed to awaken in us a desire to understand the upper worlds. We are given a greater desire to get to know our roots and to connect with them. We are then empowered to improve and fulfill ourselves.

All three great Kabbalists are of the same soul: first appearing as Rabbi Shimon, on a second occasion as the Ari, and the third time as Rabbi Yehuda Ashlag. On each occasion, the timing was ripe for further revelation because the people of that generation were worthy, and the soul descended to teach the method suitable for that generation.

Each generation is increasingly worthy of discovering The Zohar. What was written by Rabbi Shimon Bar Yochai and hidden was later discovered by the generation of Rabbi Moshe de Leon, and then by the Ari, who started to interpret it in the language of Kabbalah. These writings were also stored away and partly rediscovered when the timing was right. Our generation is privileged to learn from the Sulam, which enables everyone to study Kabbalah and to correct himself now.

We see that The Zohar speaks to each generation. In each generation it is more revealed and better understood than in the generation before. Each generation opens the book of The Zohar in a unique way, suited to the roots of its particular soul.

Importantly, at the same time, an attempt is made to conceal Kabbalistic writings so that those feeling the need to seek them will discover them by themselves. The Kabbalists evidently know that the process of change requires two conditions: correct timing and maturity of the soul. We are witnessing a very interesting occurrence, characterized by the breakthrough and signaling of a new era in the study of Kabbalah.

Chapter 5

Who Can Study Kabbalah?

Whenever Kabbalah is discussed, statements are tossed about such as: One can go mad studying Kabbalah; it is safe to study Kabbalah only after the age of 40; a man must be married and have at least three children before embarking on its study; women are forbidden to study Kabbalah, etc.

Kabbalah is open to all. It is for those who truly wish to correct themselves in order to attain spirituality. The need comes from the soul's urge to correct itself. That is actually the only test to determine whether a person is ready to study Kabbalah: the desire to correct oneself. This desire must be genuine and free of outside pressure, since only one's self can discover one's true desire.

The great Kabbalist, the Ari, wrote that from his generation onwards Kabbalah was intended for men, women and children, and that all could and should study Kabbalah. The greatest Kabbalist in our generation, Yehuda Ashlag, Baal HaSulam, left a new study method for this generation. It is suitable for anyone wishing to embark on the study of Kabbalah.

A person finds his way to Kabbalah when he is no longer satisfied by material reward and hopes studying will provide answers, clarification and new opportunities. He no longer finds solutions in this world to the significant questions concerning his existence. More often than not, the hope of finding answers is not even cognitive; he simply takes an interest and finds it necessary.

Such a person has questions: Who am I? Why was I born? Where do I come from? Where am I going? Why do I exist in the world? Was I already here? Will I reappear? Why is there so much suffering in the world? Can it somehow be avoided? How can I attain pleasure, completeness, peace of mind? Unconsciously, he feels the answers to these questions can be found only beyond the realm of this world.

The one answer to these questions is to know and feel the upper worlds, and the way to do so is through Kabbalah. Through its wisdom, man enters the upper worlds with all his feelings. They are worlds that provide all of the reasons for his existence in this world. He takes control of his life, thereby attaining his goal—tranquility, pleasure and completeness— while he is still in this world.

In the Introduction to the Study of the Ten Sefirot it is written: "If we put our hearts into answering just one famous question, I am sure all questions and doubts will disappear from the horizon and we will find they are gone. And that tiny question is—What is the point of our lives?"

Anyone attracted to the study of Kabbalah due to this question is welcome to study Kabbalah. The one who reaches serious study feels this question and asks himself constantly: "What is the point of our lives?" This is what urges him to search and find answers.

People want quick cures. They want to learn about magic, meditation and healing associated with Kabbalah. They are not truly interested in the revelation of the upper worlds, or in learning the methods of reaching spiritual realms. This does not qualify as a genuine desire to study Kabbalah.

When the time is right and the need is there, a person will look for a framework of study and will not be satisfied until he finds one. Everything depends on the root of man's soul and that point of his heart. A true desire within his heart to discover and feel the upper worlds will lead him to the way of Kabbalah.

Chapter 6

How To Study Kabbalah

Several hundred years ago, it was impossible to find Kabbalah books or books on this subject. Kabbalah was transmitted solely from one Kabbalist to another, never reaching the ordinary person. Today, the situation is reversed. There is a desire to circulate the material among all, and to call on everyone to participate in its study. When studying these books, the desire for spirituality grows, whereby the light surrounding us, the real world hidden from us, starts to reflect on those people who wish to be closer to the special charm of spirituality, and they start to desire it even more.

Kabbalists prohibited the study of Kabbalah by people who had not been prepared for it, unless they did so under special circumstances. They treated their students cautiously to ensure they studied in the proper manner. They limited students by certain criteria.

Baal HaSulam describes these reasons at the beginning of his Introduction to the Study of the Ten Sefirot. However, if we understand these restrictions as conditions for the proper comprehension of Kabbalah, we will see that they are intended as a way to prevent students from deviating from the correct way.

What has changed is that we now have more of a language, better conditions and a stronger determination to study Kabbalah. Because souls feel the need to study Kabbalah, Kabbalists such as Baal HaSulam have written commentaries that enable us to study free of errors. Everyone can now learn Kabbalah through his books.

To study Kabbalah in the proper way, it is recommended that the student focus solely on the writings of the Ari, Baal HaSulam and Rabash in their original versions.

The primary objective of Kabbalah is to achieve spirituality.

Only one thing is necessary—proper instruction. If a person studies Kabbalah in the right way, he progresses without forcing himself. There can be no coercion in spirituality.

The aim of study is for a person to discover the connection between himself and what is written in the book; this should always be borne in mind. That is the reason Kabbalists wrote down what they experienced and achieved. It is not in order to acquire knowledge of how reality is built and functions, as in science. The intention of the Kabbalah texts is to create an understanding and assimilation of its spiritual truth.

If a person approaches the texts in order to gain spirituality, the text becomes a source of light and corrects him. If he approaches the texts in order to gain wisdom, it is for him mere wisdom. The measure of inner demand is what determines the measure of strength he gleans, and the pace of his correction.

That means that if a person studies in the proper manner, he crosses the barrier between this world and the spiritual world. He enters a place of inner revelation and reaches the light. That is known as the beautiful sign. If he does not achieve this, it is a sign that he has been negligent in the quality or quantity of his efforts; he did not make a sufficient effort. It is not a question of how much he studied, but a question of how focused he was on his intentions, or if he lacked something. However, if he reaches this desire to correct himself, he can attain spirituality. Only then will the heavens open for him to allow his entry into another world, another reality, another dimension. He reaches this stage by studying Kabbalah in the right way.

Embracing Kabbalah does not work by merely avoiding nice things so that one's desire will not be kindled. Correction does not come from self-punishment, but rather as a result of spiritual achievement. When a person achieves spirituality, the light appears and corrects him.

This is the only way a person changes. Any other way is hypocritical. He is mistaken if he believes that by putting on a nice appearance he will achieve spirituality. Inner correction will not follow, since only the light can correct. The purpose of studying is to invite the light that corrects one. Therefore, a person should work on himself only for that purpose.

If there is any pressure, or any obligatory rules or regulations, it is a sign that it is man-made and is not an action intended by the upper worlds. In addition, inner harmony and tranquility are not prerequisites for attaining spirituality; they will appear as a result of the correction. But a person should not believe this can happen without an effort on his part.

The Kabbalah way absolutely rejects any form of coercion. It grants a person an inkling of spirituality, bringing him to prefer it to materialism. Then, in relation to his spirituality, he clarifies his desire. Accordingly, he retreats from material things as his attraction to or necessity for them disappears.

Studying Kabbalah incorrectly, even with the best intentions, can distance a person from spirituality. This type of student will only fail.

Among the languages of the study of spiritual worlds, between the Bible (which includes the Five Books of Moses, the Prophets and the Scriptures) and Kabbalah, the latter is the most useful and direct. Those who learn it cannot err in their understanding. It does not use names from this world, but possesses a special dictionary directly indicating the spiritual tools for spiritual objects and forces, and the correlation between them.

It is therefore the most useful language for the student to make inner progress and to correct himself. If we study the writings of Baal HaSulam, there is no danger of becoming confused.

Spirituality can be attained by studying the right books, i. e., books written by a true Kabbalist. The Bible's texts are Kabbalah texts. They are books Kabbalists wrote to one another to exchange ideas and to assist each other in learning. A person whose spiritual feelings have grown can see how these books assist him in continuing his growth and development. It is like being led by a tour guide in a foreign country. With the aid of the guidebook, the traveler becomes oriented and better understands his new whereabouts.

We need books that are suited to our souls, books by the Kabbalists of our generation or the previous one, since different souls descend in each generation and require different teaching methods.

A student in search of a Kabbalah teacher must do so with care. There are so-called Kabbalists who teach incorrectly. For example, it is sometimes claimed that wherever the word "body" is written it refers to our physical body, that the right hand symbolizes charity and the left, bravery. This is exactly the strict prohibition rendered by the Bible and Kabbalists in "Thou shall not make a sculpture or a picture."

Why are there those who teach and interpret this way? First of all, they themselves do not comprehend the kabbalistic language of branches. [See the chapter on "The Language Of Kabbalists: Branches."] If there were a direct connection between spiritual forces and our physical bodies, it would have been possible to teach people to succeed in life, and to cure the body by physical means under the guise of spirituality.

It is important to join the right study group in which to explore the writings of a real Kabbalist. This should be done under the guidance of a Kabbalist.

The group provides strength. Everybody has at least a small desire for materialism, and an even smaller desire for spiritualism. The way to augment the will for spiritualism is through joint desire. Several students together stimulate *Ohr makif* (Surrounding Light). Although the physical body separates people, it does not affect spiritualism, since in spiritualism, the point of the heart is shared by all, resulting in a much greater result.

All of the Kabbalists studied in groups. Rabbi Shimon Bar Yochai held a group for students, and so did the Ari. A group is vital in order to progress. It is the primary tool of Kabbalah, and everyone is measured by his contribution to the group.

It is essential to receive from a true Kabbalist who himself studied under the guidance of a Kabbalist. A group does not eliminate the need for a Kabbalist; it is impossible without a Kabbalist since it is he who directs the group.

The texts and the Kabbalist help the student so that he does not deviate from the correct way of studying. He works on himself and on his inner being. No one knows the others' place in the group, nor his level of spirituality. The books, the group and the Kabbalist simply help him to stay on course and increase his will for spirituality, instead of following other desires or worthless endeavors.

To help students avoid failure, a list of questions and answers and an index of words and expressions is provided. During study sessions, attention is drawn to spiritual truth, not to the depth or measure of comprehension. What is important is that the student is motivated to make spiritual progress, and not merely to advance intellectually.

It is true that people are attracted to the wisdom of Kabbalah in the hope of becoming more successful. We are all made of the desire to receive pleasure. It is our basic makeup, but with proper instruction some of us attain spirituality and eternity. Others, without the proper instruction, live under the illusion that they have achieved something spiritual. In fact, they lose their chance of attaining spirituality in this lifetime.

Chapter 7

Spirituality and Kabbalah

Man is incapable of making a move without there being some advantage in it for him. In order to act, he must first see how he may gain from it. This gain serves as the fuel that gets him moving. The fuel is either the immediate or future gain he envisages. If a person does not feel there is any profit, he will immediately halt his actions. That is because man cannot exist without feeling he will gain something.

The Kabbalah teaches man *how* to receive. In order to attain spirituality a person must expand his will to receive. He must expand his will to absorb all worlds, including this one. This is the purpose for which he was created. It is not necessary to become a monk or ascetic, or steer away from life. On the contrary, Kabbalah obliges man to marry, bear children and work and live a full life. Nothing has to be given up; everything was created for a reason, and man need not withdraw from life.

When a person begins to study Kabbalah, he may have no spiritual feelings, and therefore he embarks on the learning process with the aid of his intellect. We are supposed to open our heart through our intellect. When the heart develops, we feel what is right and what is not, and are naturally drawn to the right decisions and actions.

The Kabbalists begin by teaching spirituality in small doses, to allow the students to expand their will to receive more light, more awareness, more spiritual feeling. Increased will brings with it a greater depth, understanding and attainment. A person then reaches the highest level of spirituality he can attain, to the roots of his soul.

Chapter 8

Reincarnation and Kabbalah

None of us are new souls; we all have accumulated experiences from previous lives in other incarnations. In each generation over the past six thousand years, souls have descended that were here on previous occasions. They are not new souls, but souls of a different kind that attained some form of spiritual development.

Souls descend to earth in a special order: They enter the world cyclically. The number of souls is not infinite; they return again and again, progressing toward correction. They are encased in new physical bodies that are more or less the same, but the types of souls that descend are different. This is referred to nowadays as reincarnation. Kabbalists use another term: the development of generations.

This intertwining, the connection of the soul and body, assists in the correction of the soul. Man is referred to as "soul," not "body." The body itself can be replaced, just as organs can now be replaced. The body is useful only in that it serves as an encasement through which the soul can work. Each generation physically resembles the previous one, but they are different from one another because each time the souls descend with the added experience of their previous lives here. They arrive with renewed strength obtained while they were in heaven.

Thus, each generation possesses different desires and goals from the previous one. This leads to the specific development of each generation. Even a generation that does not reach the desire to know true reality or God-like recognition accomplishes the task by the suffering it endures. That is its way of making progress toward true reality.

All souls are derived from one, called *Adam HaRishon* (the soul of the First Man). This does not refer to Adam as a mere personality from the Bible. It is a concept of spiritual, inner reality. Parts of the soul of the first man descend into the world, taking the form of bodies, leading to a connection between body and soul. Reality is directed in such a manner that the souls descend and correct themselves. When they enter into body form they raise their level 620 times above the level from which they began. The order in which souls descend into this reality of wearing a body goes from light to heavy.

The soul of the first man comprises many parts and many desires, some light, others heavy, based on the amount of egoism and cruelty they possess. They come into our world, the lighter ones first, the heavier ones following. Accordingly, correction requirements differ.

In their descent into the world, souls have gathered experience from their suffering. This is called the path of suffering, as this experience develops the soul. Each time it is reincarnated, it has an increased unconscious urge to seek answers to questions on its existence, its roots, and the importance of man's life.

Accordingly, there are souls that are less developed, and souls that are more so. The latter have such an enormous urge to recognize the truth that they cannot limit themselves to the confinements of this world. If they are given the right tools, the proper books and instruction, they will attain recognition of the spiritual world. Kabbalah also describes the descending souls as pure or as less refined. It is a measurement in direct proportion to how much the souls require for correction. Souls requiring a greater correction are called less refined.

As different souls descend, they require different guidance and correction, unique for that generation's souls. This is why in each generation there are people who lead us in our spiritual progress. They write books and form study groups in order to convey the method of discovery of the reality that is most suited to that generation. In this, the media age, they may appear on television, radio and most recently, on the Internet.

In the beginning (before the soul of Ari appeared), there was an era of experience gathering and perseverance in this world. The souls' existence was sufficient in order to make progress toward correction. The suffering they accumulated added urgency to their souls to relieve their suffering. The desire to leave their suffering behind was the motivating force behind the development of the generations.

That era continued until the 16th century, when the Ari appeared and wrote that from his generation onwards, men, women and children in all the nations of the world could, and were required to, engage in Kabbalah. The reason was that the time had arrived in the development of generations, in which souls descending into the world were able to recognize true reality and were ready to complete their correction by the special method the Ari had developed. They could achieve what was required of them.

Souls have but one desire—while existing within physical bodies—to return to their roots, to the level they were before their descent. Physical bodies, with their desire to receive, pull them back into this world. Man consciously wishes to rise spiritually. The great effort spent on the friction created by this dichotomy is what assists him in rising 620 times above his previous level.

If a soul does not complete its task, the next time it descends into the world, it will reincarnate more deserving of correction.

Sometimes, we believe that we should deny our desires and longing so that in the next reincarnation we will be more successful. We think we should not desire anything except a little nutrition and lying in the sun, as would a cat. However, the contrary is true since in the next round, we will be even more cruel, demanding, exacting and aggressive.

The Creator wants us to be filled with spiritual pleasure, to be complete. That is possible only through great desire. Only with a corrected desire can we truly reach the spiritual world and become strong and active. If our desire is small, while it cannot do great harm, it also cannot do much good. Desire is called corrected only when it functions out of the proper influence. It does not exist in us automatically, but is acquired while studying Kabbalah in the correct manner.

A pyramid of souls exists, based on the desire to receive. At the base of the pyramid are many souls with small desires, earthly, looking for a comfortable life in an animal-like manner: food, sex, sleep. The next layer comprises fewer souls, those with the urge to acquire wealth. These are people who are willing to invest their entire lives in making money, and who sacrifice themselves for the sake of being rich.

Next are those that will do anything to control others, to govern and reach positions of power. An even greater desire, felt by even fewer souls, is for knowledge; these are scientists and academics, who spend their lives engaged in discovering something specific. They are interested in nothing but their all-important discovery.

Located at the zenith of the pyramid is the strongest desire, developed by only a small few, for the attainment of the spiritual world. All these levels are built into the pyramid.

Man also has the same pyramid of desires within him, which he must overturn so that its sheer weight will compel him to aim for the purest desire, the infinite desire for truth. He must reject and discard all his earthly egoistic desires and put every effort and energy into increasing the desire for spirituality. He achieves this through the proper way of studying.

When a person truly wishes to increase his longing for spirituality, then the light around him, the spiritual world hidden from him, starts to reflect back on him, making him long for it even more. At this stage, group study under a Kabbalist's guidance is crucial. [See the chapter on "How To Study Kabbalah."]

A major change in the souls descending today lies in the fact that we are starting to see around us a definite desire to achieve a spiritual system. Even ordinary people are seeking something spiritual, something beyond our world.

Although this "spirituality" may include all sorts of shortcuts, magic tricks and esoteric teachings and groups promising answers to those who join them, nevertheless, it bespeaks of the search for a different reality. If a generation displays a stronger desire within the souls themselves, a new method, suited to these souls, will emerge.

In the last fifteen years there has been swift and active development in the descent of new souls. The desire of these souls is much stronger and more genuine. It is directed at achieving the real truth and nothing else.

When we truly comprehend how reality applies to us and how we are affected by it, we will cease doing that which is prohibited; we will insist on the right thing and we will do it. Then we will discover harmony between the real world and ourselves.

In the meantime, we unconsciously err, then realize we have erred. It may appear that there is no possibility of escape. That is why mankind finds itself more and more in a blind alley, mired in increasingly difficult dilemmas. We will discover that there is no alternative to recognizing the spiritual world of which we are a part. This recognition will lead us to a new situation in which we will consciously begin to act as one collective body, and not just as individuals.

All people are connected to one another in one soul, from one generation of souls to the next. We all possess collective responsibility. That is why the Kabbalist is regarded as "founder of the world." He influences the entire world, and the world influences him.

Chapter 9

The Language of
Kabbalists: Branches

When we think or feel something and wish to convey it to someone else so that he may feel it too, we use words. There is a general consensus in the use of words and their meanings; when we call something "sweet," the other person immediately understands what we mean since he imagines the same taste. Yet how closely does his conception of sweet match ours? How can we best communicate our feelings while still using words?

The feelings of Kabbalists are above our level. Nevertheless, they wish to convey to us their wonder at things that have no meaning for us. They do this through means taken from our world: often words, sometimes music notes, and on occasion, by other means.

Kabbalists write about their experiences and feelings in the upper worlds. They write about the higher forces and what they discover there. They write for other Kabbalists, since the interaction of studies between them is so essential and so fruitful. Their writings are then extended to those who haven't yet sensed spirituality, for those whose spirituality is still hidden.

Since there are no words in the spiritual world to describe their spiritual feelings, Kabbalists call these experiences branches, a word taken from our world. Therefore the language used in books on Kabbalah is called the language of branches. It is a language that borrows words from our world and uses them to identify spiritual experiences. Since everything in the spiritual world has an equivalent in the physical world, each root of the spiritual world has a name and the name of its branch. And because we cannot describe our feelings precisely and do not know how to measure or compare them, we use all kinds of auxiliary words to help.

Rabbi Yehuda Ashlag writes in his book *Talmud Esser HaSefirot* (Study of the Ten Sefirot, Part 1 Looking Inwards):

> ...the Kabbalists chose a special language that can be referred to as the "language of branches." Nothing takes place in this world that is not drawn from its roots in the spiritual world. On the contrary, everything in this world originates in the spiritual world and then descends into this world. The Kabbalists accordingly found a ready language by which they could easily convey their achievements to one another orally and in writing for future generations. They took the names of branches from the material world; each name is self-explanatory and indicates its upper root in the higher world system.

For every force and action in this world there is a force and action in the spiritual world that is its root. Each spiritual force correlates to only one force, its branch in the material world.

Of this direct correlation it is written, "There is nothing growing below that does not have an angel above urging it to grow." That is, there is nothing in our world that does not have a corresponding force in the spiritual world. Because of this direct correlation, and because spirituality does not contain names—just feelings and forces without the mantle of animal, mineral, vegetable, or speech—Kabbalists use names of branches in this world in order to define their spiritual roots by them. Baal HaSulam writes further:

With all the explanations, you will comprehend what sometimes appear in the Kabbalah books as strange terminology for the human spirit, particularly in the basic Kabbalah books, The Zohar and books by the Ari. The question arises, why did Kabbalists use such simple terminology to express these lofty ideas? The explanation is that no language in the world can reasonably be used, except for the special language of branches, based on the corresponding upper roots... It should not be surprising if strange expressions are sometimes used, since there is no choice in the matter. The matter of good cannot replace the matter of bad, and vice versa. We must always convey precisely the branch or incident showing the upper root as the occasion dictates. We must also elaborate until the exact definition is found.

In Kabbalah, the student repeats the main ideas of Kabbalistic wisdom: "place," "time," "movement," "lack," "body," "body parts" or "organs," "match," "kiss," "hug," etc., over and over again, until he feels within himself the right feeling for every idea.

A final word: It should be noted that there are some so-called instructors of Kabbalah who communicate erroneous interpretations to their students. The error stems from the fact that the Kabbalists wrote their books using the language of branches and used words from our world to express spiritual ideas. Those who do not understand the correct use of this language are mistaken. They teach that there is a connection between the body and the spiritual Vessel, for example, as if by physical actions a person is doing something spiritual. The branches are an integral part of Kabbalah and without their use, one is not learning true Kabbalah.

Chapter 10

Sensing Reality through Kabbalah

Everything we know about our world is based on man-made study. Every generation studies our world and conveys its knowledge to the following generation. Through it, each generation comprehends the sort of framework in which he should live, and what his position is in relation to other generations. In each era, mankind uses the world surrounding him.

The same process takes place in spiritualism. Every generation of Kabbalists from Abraham onwards studies and discovers the spiritual worlds. Just as in scientific research, they pass along the knowledge they have attained to future generations.

In this world we have a general sense, called the desire to receive, with five receptors, which are our five senses. When a person undergoes a correction, he attains the sixth sense, known as the spiritual sense. This sense enables him to feel the spiritual reality. It is not in the same category as the other five senses whatsoever.

Scientists, too, use only their five senses. Any instrument—precise, advanced, technical, mechanical or otherwise—we regard as "objective." But these instruments merely expand the limits of our senses so that we may hear, see, smell, taste and touch more intricately. Ultimately, it is man who examines, measures and assesses the results of research, through his five senses. Obviously, he cannot provide an exact, objective answer to what is accomplished by the senses. Kabbalah, the source of all wisdom, enables us to do this.

When starting to study reality, we discover that we cannot study or understand that which is beyond us since it is unknown and unrevealed to us. If we cannot see it or touch or taste it, we may question whether it really exists. Only Kabbalists, those who attain a higher abstract upper light beyond our senses, are able to comprehend our true reality.

Kabbalists tell us that beyond our senses there is only an abstract upper light, called the Creator. Imagine that we are in the middle of the ocean, within a sea of light. We can sense all kinds of feelings that seem to be incorporated into it, as far as our ability to comprehend allows us. We do not hear what is happening elsewhere. What we regard as hearing comes as the response of our eardrums to external stimuli. We do not know what is causing it. We simply know that our eardrum reacts from within us. We assess it internally and accept it as an external event. We do not know what is happening outside of ourselves; we merely comprehend the reaction of our senses to it.

As in the example of hearing, so it is with our other senses: sight, taste, touch and smell. That means that we can never exit our "box." Whatever we say about what is happening externally is in fact the picture we paint inside us. This restriction can never be overcome.

The study of Kabbalah can assist us in expanding the borders of our natural senses to achieve the sixth sense, through which we can become acquainted with the reality around and within us. This reality is the true reality. Through it, we will be able to experience the reaction of our senses externally. If we direct all of our five senses correctly, we will see the true picture of reality. We need merely to internalize the characteristics of the spiritual world.

It is like a radio that is able to tune into a certain wavelength. The wavelength exists outside of the radio, which receives and responds to it. This example applies to us, too. If we experience at least one tiny spark of the spiritual world, we will begin to feel it within ourselves.

During his development, the Kabbalist acquires more and more spiritual characteristics, thereby connecting to all the levels of the spiritual world, all built on the same principle. When a person studies Kabbalah, he begins to understand, to feel, to assess and work with all realities, both spiritual and material, without differentiating between them. The Kabbalist reaches the spiritual world while encased in his body in this world. He feels the two worlds without any border separating them.

Only when a person experiences this true reality can he see the reasons for what is happening to him here. He understands the consequences of his actions. He then begins to be practical for the first time, living, feeling everything and knowing what he should do with himself and his life.

Prior to this recognition he does not have the ability to know why he was born, who he is and the consequences of his actions. Everything is enclosed within the borders of the material world, and the way he enters it is also the way he leaves it.

In the meantime, we are all at the level called "This World." Our senses are equally limited; therefore, we are capable only of seeing the same picture. Baal HaSulam writes, *"All upper and lower worlds are included in man."* This is the key sentence for anyone interested in the wisdom of Kabbalah and living the reality around him. The reality around us includes upper worlds as well as this world; together, they are part of man.

For the time being, we understand this world through material, physical elements. However, we add several elements when we study, through which we discover additional elements. It allows us to see things we cannot see today.

At first our level is very low, as we are located diametrically opposite the level of the Creator. But then we start to rise from this level by correcting our desire. We then discover another reality surrounding us, although no change actually occurs. We change within ourselves, and following the change, become aware of other elements surrounding us. Later, these elements disappear and we feel everything is due solely to the Creator, the Almighty. The elements we begin to gradually discover are called worlds.

We should not try to imagine spiritual reality, but should sense it. Imagining it merely distances us from its reach. Kabbalists reach the upper worlds through their senses, just as we reach out to the material world. The worlds stand between us and the Creator, hiding Him from us. As Baal HaSulam writes, it is as if the worlds filter the light for us. We can then see reality surrounding us in a different way. In fact, we will discover that there is nothing between us and the Creator.

All these disturbances, these worlds between us, hide Him from us. They are masks placed on our senses. We do not see Him in his true form; we see only fractured elements. In Hebrew, the origin of the word *Olam* (world) is *"alama"* (concealing). Part of the light is transmitted, and part is hidden. The higher the world, the less hidden the Creator is.

Those in this world paint different pictures of reality differently. Logic dictates that reality should be uniform to everyone. Nevertheless, one hears one thing, another hears something else, one sees one thing, and another sees it differently.

Baal HaSulam illustrates this by using electricity as an example: We have in our homes an electric socket that contains abstract energy which cools, heats, creates a vacuum or pressure depending on the appliance using it, and on the ability of the appliance to utilize the electricity. Yet the energy has no form of its own, and remains abstract. The appliance reveals the potential found in the electricity.

We can say the same about the upper light, the Creator that has no form. Each person feels the Creator according to the level of his correction. At the beginning of his studies, a person can see only that his reality exists, and is unable to sense any higher force.

He gradually discovers, through using his senses, the true, expanded reality. At a more advanced stage, if he corrects all his senses according to the light around him, there will be no separation between himself and the light, between man and the Creator. It will be as if there is no difference between their characteristics. The person then achieves godliness in the real sense. Godliness is the highest level of spirituality.

How can a beginner master this science when he cannot even properly understand his teacher? The answer is very simple. It is only possible when we spiritually lift ourselves up above this world.

Only if we rid ourselves of all of the traces of material egoism and accept attaining spiritual values as our true goal. Only the longing and the passion for spirituality in our world—that is the key to the higher world.

Chapter 11

Kabbalistic Music

Rabbi Yehuda Ashlag (Baal HaSulam), author of the Sulam commentary of The Zohar, expressed his spiritual feelings through the words of his numerous published writings. Among them he wrote songs and composed melodies based on these spiritual feelings.

The music itself is based on the way a person feels in the spiritual world. What is so special about the music is that everyone can understand it, even if he has not reached the composer's spiritual level. Listening to the Baal HaSulam's music, as conveyed by his son Rabbi Baruch Ashlag, we have the opportunity to experience the spiritual sentiments of these prominent Kabbalists.

The Kabbalist achieves two polarized stages in spiritualism: agony, as a result of drifting away from the Creator, and delight, as a result of getting closer to Him. The feeling of drifting away from the Creator produces sad music, expressed by a prayer appealing for closeness. The feeling of closeness to the Creator produces joyous music, expressed by a thanksgiving prayer.

Therefore, we hear and feel two distinct moods in the music: longing and desire for unification when drifting away, and love and happiness when discovering unification. The two moods together express the Kabbalist's unification with the Creator.

The music bathes the listener in a wondrous light. We do not need to know anything about it before listening to it, since it is wordless. Yet its effect on our hearts is direct and swift. Hearing it over and over again is a special experience.

The notes are composed in adherence to Kabbalistic rules. The notes are chosen according to the way man's soul is built. The listener feels them penetrating deep within his soul, unobstructed. This happens because of the direct connection between our souls and the roots of the notes.

In 1996, 1998, and 2000, three CDs of the Baal HaSulam's and Rabash's music were recorded and published. The melodies are presented as Rabbi Michael Laitman heard them from his rabbi, Rabbi Baruch Ashlag, eldest son and follower of the ways of Baal HaSulam.

Chapter 12

FAQs About Kabbalah

We learn about Kabbalah by listening, reading, studying in groups and most importantly, asking questions and receiving answers. Following are some of the most frequently asked questions drawn from our Web site.

If you have any questions you would like us to answer, please write to info@kabbalah.info or visit our web site at www.kabbalah.info.

Q.1 I have been asking myself about my place in the world. I don't know whether Kabbalah is for me. What is Kabbalah all about and what good will it do me if I study it?

A.1 Kabbalah gives one answer to one common question: What is the essence of my life and my existence? Kabbalah is for those who have been searching for answers; these people are best suited to studying Kabbalah. Kabbalah shows man the source and thus, the purpose of his life.

Q.2 I have always thought that Kabbalah is a secret. Suddenly, Kabbalah has become the new, hot topic. How did this happen?

A.2 For thousands of years it was prohibited to disseminate Kabbalah. Only during the 20th century, when the books of the Kabbalist Rabbi Yehuda Ashlag were published, have we been afforded the possibility of studying Kabbalah without restrictions. His writings are aimed at helping people like you, those without previous knowledge of

Kabbalah. It is permissible to distribute Kabbalah widely and to teach everyone who is seeking the missing spiritual elements in his life.

Q.3 **Is it true that Rabbi Ashlag thought that Kabbalah should be taught to everyone, Jew and gentile alike? Do you think that the gentile has a place in the correction process, or is this meant for study by Jews alone? And what is the correction process all about?**

A.3 You may have read in the Bible that at the end of the correction all will know God, from the youngest to the eldest, with no regard to gender or race. The Kabbalah is about man and the desire to receive, which God created. All creatures have this desire to receive. Therefore, all who want to participate in the process of correction may do so. The correction is a process of exchanging one's intentions from egoistic to altruistic ones, i.e., from the benefit of oneself to the benefit of the Creator. It is hoped that all mankind will be involved in this process.

Q.4 **I am interested in learning more about Kabbalah. Isn't it essential for a beginning student like myself to first study the Bible, the written and the oral law for many years, before I begin learning Kabbalah, or can I start now?**

A.4 There are no prerequisite conditions to studying Kabbalah. All that is needed is one's curiosity and the will to learn. Through the study of Kabbalah one learns how to be similar to the spiritual world in one's deeds and thoughts.

Q.5 **I have heard rumors that a rabbi or Kabbalah student put a spell on someone so he would die. My questions: Is such a thing possible? And if so, is there a spell that can be said?**

Also, I have purchased several books related to "good" magical practices and would like to know if you can steer me in the right direction as far as some of these books go.

A.5 I do not know what books you have bought, but they do not deal with the true Kabbalah. Kabbalah is not about magic. Through study and reading you can gain a better understanding of Kabbalah. We recommend several types of readings, e.g., the articles we prepare in which we teach about the stages of man's development along his spiritual course. While it is important to study with a teacher and in a group setting, you can access these articles through our Web site, and special prayer books that we produce.

Q.6 Seven years ago, I began my search for God, the Creator, the Father. Along the way my entire life was destroyed and I lost everything I held dear. One day I told Him, "I will not give up until you answer me! You are all I have left." Now I have begun to experience lights around people and animals. Isn't this a manifestation of Kabbalah? I want to know God and to develop spiritually.

A.6 Your situation is precisely what motivates man to study Kabbalah. The way to know God is very difficult and requires specific study. And only after a spiritual feeling becomes revealed to him, does a man understand that his former feelings were just products of his imagination. One cannot feel God until he ascends to the upper worlds by turning all his egoistic characteristics into altruistic ones.

Q.7 I understand that the word Kabbalah is from the Hebrew verb *lekabbel*, to receive. What does this mean and what is the purpose of receiving?

A.7 In the beginning, the Creator alone existed. He created a general desire to receive. This desire to receive is called The First Man (*Adam HaRishon*). In order to enable The First Man to communicate with the Creator, the general desire to receive has been divided into many parts. The purpose of the creation is to achieve communion with the Creator, because only in such a state can man achieve fulfillment, endless tranquility and happiness.

Q.8 **Does this imply that at some time in the distant future, there will be only one man, again?**

A.8 The Kabbalah does not deal with our physical body, but only with our spiritual component. The upper world is like one creature, one soul whose parts are projected to a lower world (the one we perceive) in which we feel ourselves as distinct from each other. To explain this more simply: Because we are limited within our egoism, we feel ourselves as separated from each other, despite the fact that we are all of us actually one spiritual body. Therefore, the separation exists only within our mistaken perception, for we are all in fact one.

Q.9 **What are some of the concepts I will find in The Zohar? And who wrote The Zohar?**

A.9 The book of The Zohar explains how a man in this world can reach the source of his soul. This road, or ladder, consists of 125 steps. The author of The Zohar must have passed through all of these stages. The soul of Rabbi Yehuda Ashlag had reached the same heights (and spiritual place) as the author of The Zohar, Rabbi Shimon Bar Yochai. This is why Baal HaSulam was able to complete the commentary on The Zohar, which we can use today.

Q.10 Are you affiliated with other rabbis and other Kabbalah centers?

A.10 Bnei Baruch is not connected in any manner to any other groups or organizations that deal with Kabbalah.

Q.11 Do you have a list of books or study materials that you could send me in English, French or Spanish?

A.11 Unfortunately, there are no reputable, serious Kabbalah books written in any language other than Hebrew and Aramaic and based on authentic sources, i.e., Shimon Bar Yochai, the Ari, Yehuda Ashlag, etc. Bnei Baruch has created a basic course in Kabbalah through its Web site, and is publishing books for beginners in several languages, including Spanish, German and Russian. The latest publication by Bnei Baruch, *Attaining the Worlds Beyond*, is available in English and Russian.

Q.12 I was raised in a religion other than Judaism. It is my belief there are more gods, more holy spirits, etc., than are mentioned in Kabbalah. And isn't the purpose of creation to give man a better life in this world, as well as the world to come? I look around me and see what a terrible place this world can be.

A.12 There exists only the Creator and man. The purpose of creation is to ascend to the upper worlds while being in this world. This can be done if man's thoughts and desires are equivalent to the desires and thoughts of the upper worlds, a subject taught in Kabbalah. One who wants to ascend and reach the goal of creation (which is each man's personal goal in life, or he must return to this world after his death) must think positively about all creation.

Q.13 I am beginning to understand that I must take responsibility for my own actions, my own ego. I want to attain a more spiritual level in my life. Where do I start? And if I study Kabbalah, will I be able to act freely?

A.13 Man must always imagine that he stands in front of God, the Super Power. Everyone who studies Kabbalah and rises to a certain spiritual level can acquire such capabilities from this Super Power that allow him to use them as he wishes. And the greater his spiritual level, the more Creator-like characteristics and powers the Kabbalist achieves. Because of this, we may also say that the Kabbalist is able to act as freely and independently as the Creator. But no true Kabbalist will ever share these intimate experiences with others.

Q.14 I read somewhere that there is a portion of the Kabbalah that contains the 72 words or names for God and when read, the scripture makes known a message. Also, when the Hebrew characters are viewed vertically, they appear in columns of three characters and each column contains a word for God. I don't know if you ever noticed that God hides things in plain view, as is the case here.

A.14 Kabbalah utilizes many mathematical concepts such as matrices, geometry, numbers, graphs, characters and letters, etc. These approaches are codes, shown in the Bible, which inform us of spiritual objects and the connection between them. Each spiritual level has its own name or number equivalent based on the sum of all letters in the name. The transformation of a name to a number is called gematria. These codes refer to spiritual levels that we should attain.

Q.15 I live in London. I am not Jewish but over the past few years I have become interested in Kabbalah and have also developed an increasing, personal interest in Judaism. Are

you able to provide any guidance whereby I can increase my knowledge? Do you have any representatives/members in the U.K. whom it would be possible to meet?

A.15 There are no Kabbalists of repute living outside of Israel. However, we recommend that you begin to study, access our web site, and send us questions and requests.

Q.16 **The Kabbalah seems to have ideas similar to all the major mystical traditions, such as Buddhism. Is there an important difference? If so, why should one choose this way and not another? If there is not, why isn't it acknowledged by Kabbalists?**

A.16 The general idea of all religious and mystical teachings is to commune with an upper entity. Every person comes with his own reason for seeking communion with this entity. For example, some people wish to enjoy an enriched and happy life in this world, to merit prosperity, health, confidence, a better future. They want to understand this world as much as possible in order to better manage their lives. Others wish to learn how to manage in the world to come after death. All of these goals are selfish and arise from man's egoism.

Kabbalah does not deal at all with these reasonings. Rather, Kabbalah aims to change man's nature in order to enable him to have qualities similar to those of the Creator.

The Kabbalistic method states that man must use everything he has in this world with the intention of giving to the Creator. To reach this intention, however, man needs to sense the Creator and must feel that the Creator enjoys his deeds. One who studies Kabbalah begins to understand its meaning through the sensing of the Creator.

Part II

Ten Kabbalah Lessons

The goal of the following series of lectures is to assist you in traversing the first stages toward the apprehension of the spiritual realm.

How To Read
Kabbalistic Text

Hebrew Terms in the Lessons

We would like to point out that it is not necessary to translate Hebrew terms used in Kabbalah into another language, since each one of them designates a spiritual entity (*partzuf*) or one of its parts.

We have provided some parallel translation to assist the English-speaking student. However, it should be emphasized that translations may lead to the association with images of our world. This is strictly forbidden because one should not attempt to lower the spiritual to the level of our world.

Terms such as Head (*Rosh*), Mouth (*Peh*), Coupling (*Zivug*), etc., could induce associations that have nothing to do with Kabbalah.

Therefore, it is recommended to stick to the Hebrew denominations. Students, who do not understand Hebrew actually have an advantage over Hebrew speakers, as these terms will not bear reference to representations from our world.

How To Read the Lessons

The difficulty of explaining and teaching Kabbalah lies in the fact that the spiritual world has no counterpart in our world. Even if the objective of study becomes clear, understanding of it is only temporary. It is grasped by the spiritual component of our cognizance, which is constantly renewed from Above.

Thus, a subject once understood by an individual may again appear unclear at a later date. Depending on the mood and the spiritual state of the reader, the text can appear as either full of deep meaning, or entirely meaningless.

Do not despair if what was so clear yesterday becomes very confusing the next day. Do not give up if the text appears to be vague, strange, or illogical. Kabbalah is not studied for the sake of acquiring theoretical knowledge, but in order to see and to perceive. When a person begins to see and perceive, then, through his own contemplation and after acquiring spiritual strength, his consequent reception of the resulting spiritual lights and levels will bestow upon him a sure knowledge.

Until a person has a comprehension of the Upper Light, and a perception of spiritual objects, he will not understand in what way the universe is built and works, since there are no analogies in our own world to the subject being learned.

These lessons can help in facilitating the first steps toward perceiving the spiritual forces. At later stages, progress can be made only with the help of a teacher.

Lesson 1

Topics examined in this lesson:

Lesson 1

Our knowledge of the spiritual worlds was given by people who managed to develop a perception of the upper worlds and described the mechanisms and structures of those worlds in their writings. Methods of establishing contact with these worlds were also passed on. This legacy enables us to enter the spiritual worlds, acquire the full knowledge, perceive complete perfection, understand the goal of Creation and fully grasp our existential purpose, while still living in this world.

This course by Rabbi Michael Laitman is based on three sources: Rabbi Shimon Bar Yochai's Zohar written in the 2nd century CE, the works of the Ari, Rabbi Y. Luria, a Kabbalist who lived in Safed in the 16th century, and finally, the works of Rabbi Yehuda Ashlag (the Baal HaSulam), who lived in the middle of the 20th century.

These three Kabbalists are one and the same soul which reincarnated several times to teach an updated method leading to the mastery of the spiritual worlds, thereby easing the study of Kabbalah for the following generations.

This unique soul reached its highest level during its last incarnation, giving life to Rabbi Yehuda Ashlag, the Baal HaSulam. During its journey through our world this soul was able to provide explanations on the structure of the spiritual worlds beginning with the highest degrees, from the birth of the first being up to the completion of the correction of the universe.

Rabbi Yehuda Ashlag explains that the "Light emanating from the Creator" designates the desire to create beings and to please them. This phase is referred to as the Root Phase or Phase 0. In Hebrew, it is called *Behina Shoresh* or *Keter*, as shown in Figure 1.

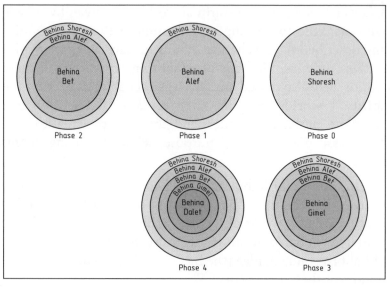

Figure 1. Five *Behinot*

Afterwards this Light creates a Vessel whose desire to receive pleasure perfectly matches it. The Light fills up the Vessel and pleases it. This is Phase 1, *Behina Alef* or *Hochma*.

The attribute of this Light is to give, to bear the delight, while the attribute of the Vessels consists in receiving, experiencing pleasure. However, when the Light enters the Vessel, it begins to transfer to the Vessel its attributes and the Vessel wishes to become like the Light; instead of wanting to receive, it now wants to give without restraint. At this stage, the Vessel desires to be like the Light, i.e. to give without restraint, and therefore it refuses to receive because it has nothing to give. This stage is called Phase 2, *Behina Bet* or *Bina*.

Being empty of the Light, the Vessel begins to consider that the goal of the Light consists in creating a Vessel and pleasing it. Clearly, the Vessel can only experience pleasure if it receives a certain portion of the Light.

The next phase corresponds to the desire to receive, let us say, ten percent of the Light, pleasure, but with an intention turned toward the Creator (bestowal). This process is in fact a mixed phase, Phase 3, *Behina Gimel* or *Zeir Anpin*.

After having reached this state, consisting of these two antagonistic elements, the "Vessel-Desire" realizes that it is more natural and better to receive than to give, to give without restraint. The original attribute of receiving and enjoying is rekindled. The Light of *Hassadim*, which has only filled ten percent of the Vessel, cannot transfer to the Vessel the attribute of giving without restraint, which thus leads to the predominance of the original attribute of receiving.

As a result, the Vessel decides that it must fill itself with one hundred percent pleasure, receive the entire Light. This is Phase 4, *Behina Dalet* or *Malchut*. Such a completely filled Vessel is defined as a true, genuine creation since its desires come from within itself, which is different from Phase 1, in that it had no independent desires of its own, being filled with the Light because the Creator so wished.

Only at Phase 4 the true choice to receive the Light emanating from the Creator is made by the created being itself. This first desire, to receive pleasure from the Light, is born inside the created being.

As shown in Figure 2, *Hochma, Bina, Zeir Anpin* and *Malchut* are the four phases of emanation of Light. The Light of *Keter* emanating from the Creator is meant to form the desire to receive, or the true creation.

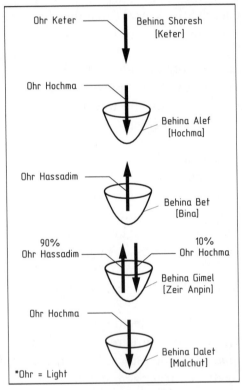

Figure 2. Four Phases of Emanation of Light

There is nothing in the world except for the Creator's desire to please and the created being's desire to receive that pleasure. Everything is ruled by it. The entire creation in all its possible stages of development: inanimate, vegetative, animate and speaking—everything desires to receive a spark of the Light, to receive pleasure.

The Creator has brought forth the Creation so that upon receiving the Light it may experience infinite and everlasting pleasure, not in a selfish way, but rather in a perfect and an absolute way. If the Light enters the Vessel and fills it up completely, then this Vessel can no longer receive because the desire is saturated by the Light, and in the absence of a desire the pleasure passes away as well.

It is only possible to receive endlessly when you do not receive for your own sake, i.e. you enjoy for the sake of the giver. Then the Light entering the Vessel does not neutralize the desire to receive.

Through experience we all know that when we are hungry and begin to eat, after a certain time we no longer feel the hunger even if the most delicious dishes are made available.

Pleasure is experienced on the borderline between pleasure itself and the desire for it. However, as soon as pleasure enters the desire and starts to satisfy it, this desire slowly fades away. And if the pleasure is stronger than the desire this can even lead to repulsion.

How can pleasure be converted into something perfect and unbounded? A specific scheme has been devised by the Creator. If man feels pleasure not within himself, but while pleasing others, this pleasure is infinite because it depends solely on the amount of pleasure he can still give and to whom he is giving it. The more people I give it to the more pleasure do I feel myself. This condition produces an eternal existence, the perfection, which is one of the attributes of the Creator. This is exactly the state the Creator wants to usher us into.

If the created being wishes exclusively to receive, it finds itself trapped in a vicious circle. It can feel only whatever is inside of it. If the created being could feel the Creator's pleasure from delighting the creation, it would endlessly experience the pleasure, just like a mother, who selflessly gives to her children.

The optimal scheme corresponds to perfection. The Light does not only transmit simple pleasure, but includes pleasure procured by unlimited knowledge, infinite existence, self-knowledge and self-analysis, a feeling of eternity and harmony, which pervades everything.

The ideal scheme includes the Creator relentlessly pouring the Light on the created being. The created being consents to receive the Light only if by doing so it pleases the Creator. This system is referred to as Returned Light or Reflected Light, as opposed to the Straight Light emanating from the Creator.

For this scheme to be, there must exist first and foremost a desire that attracts the Straight Light towards the created being. Secondly, the created being must place a Screen on the Light's path. This Screen prevents the experiencing of pleasure for one's own sake and enables the created being to receive pleasure, but only in proportion to what he can give for the sake of the Creator. Then the created being becomes completely like the Creator.

In other words, the following exchange takes place: the Creator procures pleasure to the created being who accepts it under the exclusive condition that by doing so it pleases the Creator.

The Baal HaSulam quotes the very simple and eternal example of the guest and the host. The host presents to his guest a table full of delicacies. The guest sits down but dares not eat because he does not want to be in a position to receive and he is not certain if the host is sincere in his desire to delight him. The guest is embarrassed because he has only to receive while the host gives. That is why the guest refuses what is offered in order to understand the host's true desire.

If the host insists, asking his guest to honor the food and assuring him that he will be very pleased if he does so, then the guest will start eating. He will do so because he is convinced that this will please the host and he no longer feels that he is receiving from the host but giving to him, i.e., he gives him pleasure.

The roles have been reversed. Even if it is the host who has prepared all the food and acts as the inviter, he clearly understands that the fulfillment of his desire to please depends uniquely on his guest. The guest holds the key to the success of the dinner and consequently masters the situation.

The Creator has especially made the created being in such a way that under the influence of the Light it will feel ashamed of only receiving. The created being, using its freedom of choice freely, will reach a level where pleasure is not experienced selfishly, so as to please the Creator. In this case the created being equals the Creator; *Malchut* rises to the level of *Keter* and acquires divine attributes.

These divine attributes, these feelings are beyond description and we cannot conceive them. The entrance into the spiritual worlds by acquiring just one degree of similitude with the Creator already means eternity, absolute pleasure and attainment.

The science of Kabbalah studies the unfolding of Creation. It describes the path along which our world and all other worlds, the whole universe, must tread while achieving their progressive correction (*Tikkun*) to reach the level of the

Creator, the ultimate degree of perfection and eternity. We need to undertake this work of correction while living in this world, in our everyday circumstances and dressed in our body.

Kabbalists have reached this degree of perfection and described it for us. All souls without exception must reach this ultimate level in due time. The reincarnation of souls in our world will carry on until the last soul has completed its way. It is only our world where the correction is possible in order to later on enter the spiritual world and eventually reach the zero-point, or *Keter*.

Could this process take place in one single life? No, that is impossible. When a person is born, he receives a soul that has already been in this world. This soul has experienced certain stages of correction and gained experience. That's why the people born today are much smarter and have more experience than previous generations. They are more prepared to function under modern technological and cultural conditions, various transformations taking place in modern society. In our generation, the desire to study Kabbalah has become more and more popular. Souls have gained such a level of experience and reached such an understanding during past lives that a 20 to 25-year-old person cannot proceed without spiritual knowledge. In the past, on the other hand, only a handful amongst millions vaguely felt the need for spirituality.

In a few years only, it will be possible to reach spiritual attainment during one's lifetime. This is the goal of creation; it has been predetermined. Each one of us is a fragment of the one and same *Malchut* (the original soul) and we are endowed with particular attributes and a specific part to play in this world. By transforming its attributes with the help of the scientific system of Kabbalah, each fragment performs its correction in order to reach its highest degree.

The fragment's path is predefined from Above. We are all born in this world with a certain soul and specific qualities. None of us have chosen our soul in advance. It goes without saying that our path is also predetermined. So what are we to do? Where is our free will? In what way are we intelligent beings and not simply mechanical elements upon which such and such actions are carried out? To what extent did the Creator retreat to allow us to express ourselves? He did it by requiring one important condition: a man has to wish by himself to advance on the path of correction and elevation and may push himself in proportion to the strength with which he stimulates his own desires.

Each one of us has to start from the starting point and eventually reach the final point. There is no free will for this. There is also no free will for the path because everyone has to go through all its phases and feelings and progressively integrate them in himself. In other words, we must "live" the path.

Freedom means being in agreement with what happens all along the path, justifying each step and selecting the maximum speed to undergo the process of correction and bonding with the Creator. This is the only human-dependent factor and this is where the essence of creation lies. To wish by himself to most quickly get rid of the initial condition, the way the Creator created him, to undergo a correction of attributes, and in the final point to bond to the Creator.

Depending on how much man expresses this desire he may be called a man; otherwise he is a totally impersonal creature. Kabbalah is the only science that helps man to develop and be an independent, individual, truly free personality.

The four phases leading to the formation of a *Kli* (Vessel) can be differentiated by their desire to delight (*Aviut*, thickness or coarseness). In Phase 0 (Root Phase) and

Phase 1 this desire is absent. The more remotely the created being stands from the Creator, the stronger the desire to delight, the coarser, the more selfish it is, the more it wants to receive.

The fourth phase, *Malchut*, is absolutely selfish, and this desire stems from its own decision. Each subsequent phase contains the previous one: *Keter* is in *Hochma*, both are then contained in *Bina*, the three are in *Zeir Anpin*. *Malchut* comprises the four previous phases. Every previous phase supports the next one and provides its existence.

The fourth phase has received all the Light, which filled it completely. We know that when the Light fills the Vessel with pleasure, the Vessel gradually receives from the Light its attribute to give. *Malchut* then begins to feel that its attribute is completely opposite to the attribute of the Light. It becomes aware of its selfishness compared to the giver, which breeds such a feeling of shame that it decides to stop receiving Light and remains empty.

The rejection of the Light from *Malchut* is called *Tzimtzum Alef*, the First Restriction. Once *Malchut* is empty, a state of equilibrium with the giver sets in; neither of them receives or gives, there is no reciprocal pleasure. So how can *Malchut* possibly equal the Creator?

By imitating the example of the guest and the host, *Malchut* pushes away all the incoming Light because it does not want to feel as the receiver. Then it sets the condition that it will accept a portion of the Light, though not for its own delight, but because it wants to please the Creator, as it knows that the Creator wishes its delight. Receiving in such a way is like giving, so *Malchut* is now in a position to be the giver.

We can see that the Light needs to undergo four phases if a true desire is to be brought to life. The same process takes place with all our desires whatever they are. Prior to the manifestation of a desire within us, this desire goes through all the phases of development of Light emanating from the Creator, until we finally feel it. No desire can emerge without Light. Light comes first, the desire afterwards.

Let us examine the structure of Creation created during Phase 4 (see Figure 3). The Light emanating from the Creator is called Straight Light (*Ohr Yashar*), the Light *Malchut* pushes away is called the Reflected Light (*Ohr Hozer*) and finally the Light entering partially into the Vessel is called Inner Light (*Ohr Pnimi*).

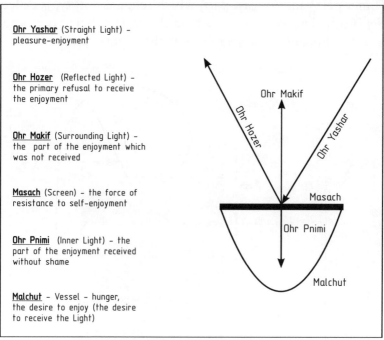

Ohr Yashar (Straight Light) – pleasure-enjoyment

Ohr Hozer (Reflected Light) – the primary refusal to receive the enjoyment

Ohr Makif (Surrounding Light) – the part of the enjoyment which was not received

Masach (Screen) – the force of resistance to self-enjoyment

Ohr Pnimi (Inner Light) – the part of the enjoyment received without shame

Malchut – Vessel – hunger, the desire to enjoy (the desire to receive the Light)

Figure 3. The Vessel

When the guest faces the host and the table full of delicacies he first refuses everything, then decides to eat a bit in order to please the host even though he would like to gulp everything down in one go. This means that one must use his selfish desires, but in an altruistic way. As the guest starts to consider things, he understands that he cannot accept the whole dinner for the sake of the host; he only may accept a small portion of it.

This is why the created being, after having performed a restriction, can accept with altruism a small portion of the Light, let's say 20%, but it pushes away the remaining 80%. The part of the created being that makes a decision on how much Light it may accept inside for the sake of the Creator is called *Rosh* (Head). The part accepting the Light is called *Toch* (Inner part) and the last part, which remains empty, is called *Sof* (End). This is the place where the created being performs a restriction and no longer accepts the Light.

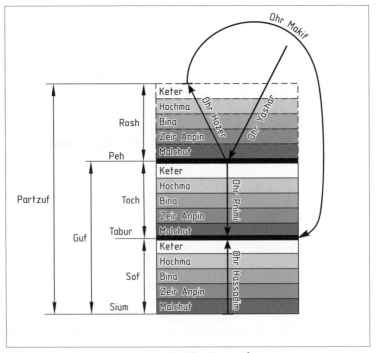

Figure 4. The *Partzuf*

Different terms are attributed to the various parts of creation using analogies with the human body. There are no terms, labels and numbers in the spiritual worlds. It is nevertheless easier and more convenient to use words.

Kabbalists have chosen to express themselves in a very simple language: given the fact that everything in our world results from the spiritual worlds, in accordance with the direct connections descending from Above downward, from every spiritual object to every object in our world. Then for everything that has a name in our world, we may take the name of an object of our world and use it to designate the spiritual object that begets it.

Let's take the example of a stone in our world. There is a force Above which generates this stone: it will therefore be named "stone." The only difference is that the "spiritual stone" is a spiritual root endowed with specific attributes, which in turn matches a branch in our world, labeled "stone," a material object. This is how the language of branches was created. By means of names, denominations and actions of our world we can refer back to elements and actions in the spiritual worlds.

None of the authentic Kabbalah scripts mention our world, not in a single word, although they may be using the language of our world. Every object of our world refers to a matching object in the spiritual worlds.

Hence the region of a spiritual object responsible for analysis and consideration is called Head (*Rosh*), see Figure 4. The part of the Screen located above *Malchut* and which lets the Light enter inside is called Mouth (*Peh*). The part where the Light enters is called Body (*Guf*). The line exerting a restriction, inside the *Guf*, is called Navel (*Tabur*). The lowest part, which is devoid of Light, is called Conclusion (*Sium*). This object as a whole constitutes the Creation, the soul, *Malchut*.

Thus, after having received twenty percent of the Light in *Toch*, the region of *Guf* where the light is actually felt, the *Partzuf* begins to feel the pressure exerted from outside by the Surrounding Light, the *Ohr Makif*. It says: "You see how pleasant it is to accept a portion of the Light, you do not know how much pleasure remains outside, just try to accept some more." We can understand that it is better not to experience pleasure at all than to experience just a tiny bit of it. Pleasure exerts pressure both from outside and inside and it therefore becomes much more difficult to oppose.

While it was not accepting any Light at all, the *Partzuf* could remain in that state for a long time, but now the Light exerts pressure both from inside and outside. If the *Partzuf* accepts some more Light, this means acting for its own delight, because the strength of its resistance to selfishness equals only twenty percent. The *Partzuf* declines to do so. It did perform the First Restriction, not to act later on in such a way. This would be totally inappropriate. There is only a single solution, which consists in rejecting the Light in order to revert to the initial state, the way it was before accepting the Light (see Figure 4). And this is exactly what the *Partzuf* does.

The pressure exerted simultaneously by the *Ohr Pnimi* and the *Ohr Makif* on the *Tabur* is termed "*Bitush Pnim uMakif*" (Blow from Inside and Outside).

How does the spreading of the Light (twenty percent in this case) inside the *Guf* take place? The Screen, which was initially positioned on the level of *Peh de Rosh* (the Mouth of the Head), is brought down by the Light's pressure by twenty percent below the *Peh* into the *Guf*, until it reaches the line of the *Tabur*.

When the Light is expelled from the *Guf*, the Screen rises progressively from the *Tabur* to the *Peh de Rosh*, pushing the Light away. Before the spreading of the Light inside the *Guf*, the *Partzuf* had all information available in the *Rosh*. It knew what kind of Light it is, what kind of delight it brings, it knew what its own desire is, and how strong its force is opposed to the delight for its own sake.

According to all this information, as well as the information remaining from the state when the *Partzuf* was filled with Light, and from the state following the restriction of the Light, the *Partzuf* keeps a memory of the past—an imprint, which is called *Reshimo*.

What exists in the spiritual? Nothing but the desire to delight and the delights satisfying this desire. The information about the desire per se in the *Partzuf* is called *Aviut*, and the information corresponding to the Light, which would clothe itself with a *Kli* (Vessel), is called *Hitlabshut*. One can justly say that there is only the Creator and Creation.

From the previous state there always remain a *Reshimo* of *Hitlabshut* and a *Reshimo* of *Aviut*. These two parameters are sufficient to define the previous state of the *Partzuf*. After having rejected the Light, a *Partzuf* knows precisely what it felt when the Light resided in its *Guf*. With this experience it knows how to act and what sort of calculations it has to carry out.

The *Partzuf*, shown in Figure 5, understands that it is no longer possible to retain twenty percent of the Light. The decision is made to taste fifteen percent of it for the sake of the Creator.

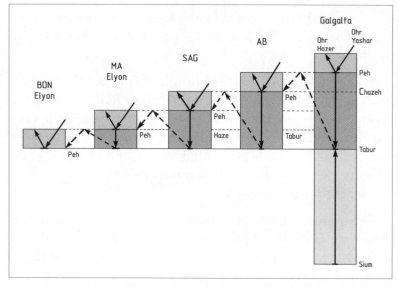

Figure 5. Five Partzufim: *Galgalta, AB, SAG, MA, BON*

For this to happen, the *Partzuf* needs to move down a bit so that its *Rosh* and *Peh* will be positioned below the level of the previous *Partzuf*. The Light hitting the Screen is pushed away, and only perhaps fifteen percent gets in.

How are the *Hitlabshut* and the *Aviut* determined? The calculation begins in the World of *Ein Sof* (the World of Infinity), where *Malchut* (*Aviut Dalet*, Desire of Level 4) is totally filled with the corresponding Light (*Hitlabshut Dalet*, Light of Level 4). This state of *Malchut* is shortly characterized by *"Dalet-Dalet,"* and is denoted by (4,4).

The next *Partzuf* retains the data that now it is capable to fill itself up with Light, which corresponds only to *Aviut Gimel*, Desire of Level 3, and so on.

Each of the following *Partzufim* lowers its capacity to fill its *Guf* with Light for the sake of the Creator more and more.

Altogether there are 25 *Partzufim*, which emerge from above to below. When the turn of the last *Partzuf* arrives, its lower part crosses the separating line, the Barrier (*Machsom*) between the spiritual world and our world, and begins to shine in our world. Our world is a state of *Malchut* characterized by the absence of a Screen.

Lesson 2

Topics examined in this lesson:

1. The Goal of Creation
2. Inanimate, Vegetative, Animate, Speaking
3. Comprehending the Spiritual Laws
4. Delight
5. Two Steps in Comprehension
6. Receiving and Giving
7. The Spiritual Shame
8. *Hitlabshut* and *Aviut*
9. The *Bitush Pnim uMakif*
10. Five Parts of *Adam Kadmon*

Lesson 2

Man was created for receiving unlimited and absolute Delight. But to reach such a condition man needs to know how the system of worlds operates.

The laws of this world are issued from the spiritual worlds. There our souls were before our birth, and there our souls return after life.

We are interested only in this particular time period when we are in our physical body and how Kabbalah can teach us the best way to live this life.

Kabbalah tells us how to use to its fullest everything that happens to us. To ascend spiritually, man needs to know everything and use absolutely all the possibilities he is offered.

We have to grasp the nature of our world: inanimate, vegetative, animate and speaking. We need to understand our soul, as well as the laws that describe its development.

According to the law of spiritual development, man has to reach the highest spiritual degree in this life. Man will be given many opportunities, if not in his present life then in the next one, and so on, until he reaches the required level.

Kabbalah helps us to accelerate this process. The Creator designed a very interesting system: either man accepts to ponder the meaning of life without awaiting any sufferings, or such sufferings will be sent to him so that he may be coerced into asking himself questions.

In other words, no matter whether man progresses towards the goal of Creation voluntarily or by force, Kabbalah assists him to advance by his own will. This is the optimal way and man may enjoy it while advancing.

There are those who pose the question: Can Kabbalah help cover a mortgage loan, assist one in business, to be successful in family matters, and so on?

Actually, Kabbalah does not give an unambiguous answer on these questions. Kabbalah teaches us how to use our entire world, in the most effective way, for the achievement of the goal of creation. This is the direction in which the Creator pushes us, using all these troubles.

Kabbalah explains what spiritual load a man must take out of his life. Not how to solve our problems, but how to find a solution to the very problem for which all our everyday problems are sent to us. Suffering is just put in our way to bring us to our spiritual ascent.

When man discovers all the laws of the spiritual worlds, he knows what is sent to him from above and why, how to use these challenges in the most optimal way and how to behave correctly.

We basically do not grasp what to do when something befalls us—where to run, who to call? Solving our daily problems straightforwardly, trying to escape them as we are used to doing, will not advance us to the goal but will create new difficulties. These will only disappear when their purpose is fulfilled by drawing us closer to the goal of creation.

By knowing the spiritual laws, we are enabled to see all the causes and consequences. We observe everything through the correct perspective, we see all the links.

This way each of our steps becomes a conscious one. Life changes and no longer seems to lead to a dead end. We join together all our conditions prior to birth, during our present lifetime, and after we leave this world. We reach a completely new level of existence.

Currently, many people are beginning to think about the meaning of life and other spiritual matters. This happens because of the past experiences that have accumulated in their souls during their previous lifetimes.

The Creator sends suffering in order to allow man to meditate on the essence of these sufferings and their origin. Thus, man is able to call upon the Creator, still without understanding it. The Creator expects us to cultivate the desire to bond with Him.

However, when man takes the correct guidebook in his hands, he may progress through assiduous study, without being coerced by sufferings.

By choosing the correct path, man feels the same suffering as pleasure; he progresses more quickly and gets ahead of it, while comprehending its purpose and origin.

Thus the Creator turns into a source of delight rather than, as previously, being the source of suffering. The pace of our advancement along this path depends solely on us.

The Creator created delight for us, but in order to make us use it correctly, he has to urge us on. Striving for a pleasure that cannot be reached makes us suffer. We are ready to run after it, wherever it is.

In other words, suffering is the absence of satisfaction. But no chase after delight will bring anything good. The moment we receive it, we lose interest in it and we jump over to something else.

Delight vanishes the moment we receive it. It is impossible for suffering to be filled with delight in our world. We sense delight only on the edge between suffering and delight, when the first sensation is felt. The pursuit of satisfaction increasingly tarnishes delight.

This method of being satisfied is perverted and unfit. In order to receive eternal delight, we need to learn how to give to somebody. Knowing that the Creator wants to delight us is our only reason for experiencing it, so that we can please Him and not seek self-satisfaction.

We need to receive for the sake of giving.

It is difficult, almost impossible to speak about this process for the lack of words. Proper understanding comes only when the Creator reveals Himself.

People begin to sense the Creator after crossing the *Machsom*—the Barrier between our world and the spiritual worlds. That comes 6,000 steps before *Gmar Tikkun*—Final Correction. Each spiritual step presents a degree of the Creator's unveiling.

Final Correction follows the correction of all man's desires.

The first stage in studying Kabbalah consists in reading as many pertinent books as possible and "digesting" as much knowledge as possible.

The next stage is group work, when the student's and group's desires merge. The student's Vessel enlarges proportionately to the number of group members.

Man starts feeling outside of his individual interests. In our case it is the group that symbolizes the Creator, since everything located outside man is the Creator. Nothing exists except for the Creator and oneself. Basically, all spiritual work both starts and ends within the framework of a group.

Throughout time, Kabbalists have had groups. Only within the framework of a group and based on the mutual ties fostered by its members can students advance in their understanding of the spiritual worlds.

Gmar Tikkun is the condition when all of mankind turns into one single Kabbalistic group.

There is still a long way to go, although every day it becomes more realistic. In any event, at the highest spiritual levels everything is ready for this attainment—all the roots, all the forces.

In general we study two stages: (i) the descent of the created being from above, while it develops from the very idea, as conceived by the Creator, up to the level of our world and (ii) the ascent of man from our world all the way to the highest degree. We do not mean any actual physical movement, because our body remains on this material plane, but in a spiritual way, as a result of our efforts and development.

In the *Partzuf* shown in Figure 4 there are two conditions: (i) when it receives Light and enjoys, this *Kli* (Vessel) is called *Hochma.* (ii) when the *Kli* wants to give and also enjoys, then it is called *Bina.* These two Vessels are opposite.

In fact there also exists a third condition, the mixed one. This is where the Vessel receives a portion for the Creator's sake but still remains partly empty. Such a condition is called *Zeir Anpin.* Here we have 10% of the Light of *Hochma* and 90% of the Light of *Hassadim.*

If there is Light of *Hochma* in the Vessel, such a condition is called *Panim* (Face). It is small or big, depending on the quantity of the Light of *Hochma.*

The final stage, *Malchut,* is the genuine desire to receive—the created being—because it is eager to receive the Light of *Hochma.*

The Light therefore completely fills *Malchut.* This condition of *Malchut* is called *Ein Sof,* the World of Infinity, i.e., unlimited receiving.

Afterwards, *Malchut*, still willing to receive the Light, decides not to use this will. It understands that desire to receive for its own sake moves it away from the Creator. Therefore it makes its First Restriction and pushes the Light away and remains empty.

By giving the Light away, *Malchut* likens its attributes to the Creator's.

The delight of giving away is felt as absolute and complete. The delight does not disappear because the giver endlessly feels the receiver while giving to him and thus sending him pleasure. While doing so the *Kli* is able to endlessly feel the delight with regards to both quantity and quality.

It is understood that when the Creator created Vessels, He organized them in such a way that they progressively absorbed the Light's attribute of giving relentlessly and thereby became similar to the Light.

One may pose the question, how can *Malchut* be similar to the Light and still receive delight?

We stated previously that *Malchut* puts an anti-egoistic Screen on all its desires. One hundred percent of Light-Delight is placed in front of it, according to *Malchut*'s desire to receive, e.g. 100 kg. Using a Screen of 100 kg (the force that counteracts its wish to receive Delight), *Malchut* pushes away all the Delight and decides to receive as much Light as necessary to please the Creator.

Such receiving of Light is equal to giving without restraint.

The Light which comes to *Malchut* is called *Ohr Yashar* (Straight Light). All the Light which is reflected is called *Ohr Hozer* (Returning Light). The twenty percent of the Light which enters inside is called *Ohr Pnimi* (Inner Light).

The greatest part of the Light left outside is called *Ohr Makif* (Surrounding Light). In the lower part of *Malchut*, where *Ohr Hochma* has not entered, there is *Ohr Hassadim*.

From the condition of *Malchut* in the World of *Ein Sof*, there remains a *Reshimo*. This *Reshimo* is composed of: (i) *Dalet de Hitlabshut* (information about the quality and quantity of Light) and (ii) *Dalet de Aviut* (information about the force of desire).

Using these two kinds of memory, *Malchut* carries out the calculation in its *Rosh* that it is able to receive the first twenty percent of Light for the sake of the Creator.

In order to feel the spiritual shame resulting from receiving, without giving in return, it is necessary first of all to perceive the Creator, His properties, to feel Him as the Giver, to see His glory. Then the comparison between His properties and one's egoistic nature will bring about the feeling of shame.

But in order to arrive at this perception, one has a lot to learn. As the glory of the Creator gradually unfolds, a desire to do something for Him appears.

To give to the Superior is like receiving. We may also observe this in our world. If someone has the opportunity to do a favor to a great person, he will do it with pleasure and enjoyment.

The aim of all our work is the revelation of the Creator: His Glory and Might. Once this level is reached, what we witness will serve us as the source of energy in order to do something for the Creator's benefit.

This revelation of the Creator, it should be emphasized, will occur only when a man has already acquired a definite desire to use it only for altruistic purpose, i.e., for attaining the altruistic attributes.

The first *Partzuf* that received a portion of the Light is called *Galgalta*. After *Bitush Pnim uMakif* i.e., being struck by both Lights, *Ohr Pnimi* and *Ohr Makif*, on the Screen at the *Tabur* (Navel), the *Partzuf* realizes that it will not be able to resist the delights of the Light that presses from outside.

The *Partzuf* decides to push the Light away. In the current state this decision does not pose any problem because none of the delights are felt by the *Partzuf*.

After the forcing out of the Light, the Screen rises, weakens and joins the *Peh* (Mouth) of *Rosh* (Head). This action is called *Hizdakchut* (Refinement).

When, on the contrary, under the effect of the Light the Screen goes down, its *Aviut* (coarseness) increases.

After the forcing out of the Light from the first *Partzuf*, there remained *Reshimot*: *Dalet de Hitlabshut* (information about the quality and quantity of Light) and *Gimel de Aviut* (information about the force of desire). One measure of *Aviut* disappeared, because the *Partzuf* realized that it is impossible to work with the former degree of *Dalet*.

According to *Aviut Gimel*, the Screen descends from *Peh de Rosh* to the level lower than that of *Aviut Dalet*. If the level of *Dalet* is *Peh* of the *Partzuf* of *Galgalta*, then the level of *Gimel* is its *Chazeh*.

Once again the Light presses the Screen from above, the Screen pushes it back, but afterwards, under the influence of the *Reshimot* (plural of *Reshimo*) it decides to accept the Light up to the *Tabur* of *Galgalta* but not beneath.

However, not even the *Partzuf* of *Galgalta* was able to receive the Light under its *Tabur*. The second *Partzuf*, which is now spreading out, is called *AB*.

Again the action of *Bitush Pnim uMakif* occurs, i.e. the forcing out of the Light, and new information, *Reshimo*, now fills the *Partzuf*.

This is *Gimel de Hitlabshut* (Light of the third level, not the fourth, as in *AB*) and *Bet de Aviut* (again the loss of one level of *Aviut* owing to *Bitush Pnim uMakif*).

That is why the Screen, which ascended initially up to the *Peh* of *AB* when the Light was pushed away, now descends to the level of *Chazeh* of *AB*.

At this point a new *Partzuf* is formed by a *Zivug* (Coupling) on the *Reshimot* of *Gimel-Bet* (3,2). The new *Partzuf* is called *SAG*.

Further on a new *Bitush Pnim uMakif* makes the Screen rise up to the *Peh de Rosh* of *SAG* with the *Reshimot* of *Bet-Alef* (2,1).

Then, according to the *Reshimot*, the Screen descends to the *Chazeh* of *SAG*, from where the fourth *Partzuf*, *MA*, comes out. Next, the fifth *Partzuf*, *BON* is formed on the *Reshimot* of *Alef-Shoresh*.

Each *Partzuf* consists of five parts: *Shoresh* (Root), *Alef* (1), *Bet* (2), *Gimel* (3) and *Dalet* (4). No desire may appear without them. This formation is a rigid system which never changes.

The last stage, *Dalet*, feels all the four previous desires, with whose help it was created by the Creator. *Dalet* gives a name to each desire, and it is those names which describe how *Dalet* sees the Creator at each moment.

This is why *Dalet* itself is called by the name of the Creator: "Yood-Hay-Vav-Hay"—Y-H-V-H. These letters will be studied comprehensively further on. It is like the skeleton of a man, it may be big or small, standing or sitting, but it remains the same thing.

If a *Partzuf* is filled with the Light of *Hochma*, it is called *AB*, but if it is filled with the Light of *Hassadim*, we call it *SAG*. All the names of the *Partzufim* are based on the combination of these two Lights.

All that is described in the Bible is nothing more than spiritual *Partzufim*, filled with either the Light of *Hochma* or the Light of *Hassadim* in different proportions.

After the birth of the five *Partzufim*: *Galgalta, AB, SAG, MA* and *BON*, all the *Reshimot* disappear. All the desires that could be filled with the Light, for the benefit of the Creator, have been exhausted.

At this stage, the Screen completely loses the ability to receive Light for the Creator and can only resist egoism without receiving anything.

We see that after the First Restriction, *Malchut* can consequently receive five portions of the Light. The birth of the five *Partzufim* is called the World of *Adam Kadmon*. *Malchut* has completed its five *Reshimot*.

We see that *Malchut* of the World of *Ein Sof* is completely filled with Light. After the First Restriction, with the help of the *Partzufim*, it will only fill partially up to the level of the *Tabur*.

The task for *Malchut* is now filling its last part for the sake of the Creator as well. This part is called *Sof* (End) and spreads from the *Tabur* to *Sium Raglin* (Conclusion of Legs).

The Creator wants to fill *Malchut* with unlimited delight. All that is needed to achieve this is to create the conditions so that *Malchut* will have the desire and the power to fill the remaining part or in other words: to send the delight back to the Creator.

In the next chapter we shall see how this process takes place.

Lesson 3

Topics examined in this lesson:

Lesson 3

*E*ven an insignificant change in our senses will significantly modify our perception of reality and our world.

Everything we sense is called the Creation. As our sensations are subjective, the picture we build is also subjective.

Scientists try to expand the limits of our senses (with microscopes, telescopes, all kinds of sensors, and so on), but all these aids do not change the essence of our perceptions.

It is as if we are imprisoned by our sensory organs. All the incoming information penetrates us through the five sensors: visual, auditory, tactual, gustatory and olfactory.

The received information undergoes some processing inside a person, is sensed and assessed following one algorithm: is it better or worse for me.

From above, we are given the opportunity to create a sixth organ of sensation. This is acquired with the help of the science of Kabbalah.

If we study it correctly, using authentic sources in a group of like-minded people and under the guidance of an authentic teacher, we can qualitatively modify our organs of sensation and discover the spiritual world and the Creator.

Kabbalah teaches that the only thing created is the desire to have pleasure and delight. Our brain is aimed only at the development of this sensation, measuring it correctly. The brain is an auxiliary appliance, nothing more.

The result of studying Kabbalah correctly is a comprehensive and thorough experience of the true universe, as clear as our present perception of our world.

The perception of both worlds gives us a full and large-scale picture, including the highest force, the Creator who rules the entire universe.

Kabbalah is talking about new sensations and feelings perceived by man; they appear not in man's brain but in his heart. The heart reacts to man's inner reactions even though it is simply a pump.

In fact our sensations—feelings—are a pure spiritual substance. The various organs that enable us to "live" them are also of a spiritual nature. The heart simply reacts, since it operates to provide energy to the body in accordance with our various reactions.

In our initial condition, we simply do not understand or perceive that something is hidden from us. Yet if during our studies we begin to appreciate this fact, it already becomes a step forward in the right direction.

Further on, we begin to perceive a higher force, which establishes contact with us, sends us different situations, and their causes and effects become clearer. This already is a certain degree of revelation.

A person begins to evaluate his own deeds in accordance with what the Creator sends him. One begins to criticize one's own actions and reactions.

He thinks "This is sent to me by the Creator so that I could let it go" or "In this case I have to behave differently." Such self-criticism transports a man to the level of "Man" because he has become more than merely the two-legged creature he was before.

The man starts sensing the Creator, and sees which actions are useful to him and which are harmful.

As man sees all the due causes and effects, he begins to know what is useful and what is not. Naturally, nobody will consciously violate something while he sees what brings him a reward and what leads to a punishment.

Therefore, the revelation of the Creator grants man the opportunity to behave correctly in each specific case with maximum benefit. Such a man is then called a *tzadik*, a righteous man. He perceives the Creator, the reward for all good, as well as the additional reward for not violating a commandment.

A righteous man always justifies the Creator. When a man increasingly performs spiritual commandments, more and more light enters him. This inner light is called *Torah*.

On further revelation of the Creator, man ascends the spiritual ladder and on each rung he performs a spiritual commandment, and receives, in turn, a new portion of light.

He becomes more righteous until he reaches such a level where it is possible for him to perform commandments regardless of himself, however good or bad this might be for him.

Man sees the Creator as absolutely kind and all His actions as perfect. All this is the result of a certain degree of revelation of the Creator.

As he moves along the 6,000 steps, man realizes that everything the Creator does to him and to his fellow men stems from the desire to endlessly delight all created beings. Man is then overcome by a feeling of endless gratitude and a desire to thank the Creator through all his actions.

These actions aim at giving to the Creator. This means doing more and more to please the Creator. Such a condition is called the condition of eternal and endless love for the Creator.

At this stage man understands that the Creator only wished him good in the past. Before, when man was in his uncorrected condition, he believed that the Creator often put him in trouble, brought him grief.

The Light of the Almighty is unchanging, but when it enters an antagonistic desire it arouses an antagonistic feeling.

The spiritual world is perceived only on the edge of positive and negative conditions. One should not fear any situation that may occur.

When one commences to study Kabbalah, suddenly problems, previously unknown, begin to crop up. Without the learning of Kabbalah this would have taken a number of years. Now, the process has just been accelerated.

For this occurrence, one may use the ratio of one day for ten years. This does not mean that the number of events planned for everybody is reduced. Rather, that the speed of their occurrence is compressed over a shorter span of time.

If a student attends the group lectures and listens correctly, while lessening his ego, his pride and superficial knowledge, he will begin to delve into what he hears and pay more attention to it.

We study the process of emanation of the worlds from above to below, in order to draw the spiritual Light in relation to the material studied.

This Light gradually cleanses our Vessels, corrects them and renders them altruistic.

We have students who have been studying for ten years together with those who have commenced just a few months ago, but everyone is able to advance accordingly without hindrance.

Actually, today students come with a greater desire to understand everything; their souls are more experienced and prepared.

For the length of time you study Kabbalah is not important in itself. What is most important is to what extent the student bonds with the group's desire, how he merges with it and humbles himself with respect. Due to this bonding with the group, it is possible to reach, after a few hours, spiritual levels that would have taken years to attain through one's own efforts.

One needs to avoid pseudo-Kabbalists, religious fanatics who are miles away from true Kabbalah. One must study authentic literature only, and belong to a single group headed by one teacher.

When I discovered Kabbalah, I wanted to find out how our world, the cosmos, the planets, the stars and so on are designed. Whether there is life out in space, what the correlation is between all these aspects.

I was interested in various forms of biological life and their meaning. My specialization is biological cybernetics. I wanted to uncover the system of the regulation of organisms.

While following this path I was urged from above toward Kabbalah. As I learned more and more, I became less and less interested in such matters. I began to understand that Kabbalah does not deal with the biological body, its life and death, which are unrelated to the spiritual sphere.

The spiritual world permeates our material world and shapes everything existing in it: inanimate, vegetative, animal and human.

Thanks to Kabbalah our world can be studied correctly by understanding its spiritual roots and their interaction with it.

For example, the study of *Talmud Esser HaSefirot*, composed by the Baal HaSulam, tells us about the birth of the soul in the spiritual worlds. If one reads it word for word, it does not differ from the conception of a human being in his mother's womb, the periods of pregnancy, birth and feeding. It sounds like pure medicine.

One then begins to grasp why we perceive in our world such consequences of the spiritual laws of development. The development of the soul is explained in a language that describes the development of the body in our world.

The various types of horoscopes, astrology and predictions have nothing to do with Kabbalah. They are related to the body and its animal property to sense different things. Dogs and cats can also feel the approaching of some natural phenomena.

In present times many people rush to use so called "New Age" techniques, trying to change themselves, their lives and their destinies. Destiny may be changed, in fact, if you exert influence on your soul and learn how to control it.

When studying the laws of the spiritual world we begin to understand the laws of our world. Most sciences, such as physics, chemistry, biology, etc. become simpler and more intelligible when viewed from the viewpoint of Kabbalah.

Still, when man reaches the appropriate spiritual level, he does not care so much for material sciences, which are less organized. Substances that are spiritually organized now become of paramount interest and importance.

A Kabbalist dreams to rise above his present level but not to go down. Any Kabbalist may perceive the roots of development of all sciences, if he wishes.

The Baal HaSulam, Rabbi Ashlag, sometimes wrote about the correlation between spiritual and material sciences. A great Kabbalist, the Gaon of Vilna, enjoyed making comparisons between spiritual and material laws. He even wrote a book on geometry. Perceiving one of the highest spiritual worlds, he was able to draw a connection directly from there down to the science of our world.

As for us, having no idea of the spiritual worlds, we shall simply read these books by pronouncing words.

But even by just pronouncing these words, we are invisibly linking ourselves to the spiritual by attracting *Ohr Makif* (Surrounding Light) from a certain level where the author was. When reading the books of the genuine Kabbalists, we allow the *Ohr Makif* to drive us forward.

The diversity of levels and types of Kabbalist souls accounts for the variety of styles expressed in Kabbalistic works, as well as the various degrees of Light intensity we may draw while studying them.

However, the Light emanating from the various books of the Torah, and amongst them, from its special part, Kabbalah, does always exist.

The Kabbalist Moses wrote a book about the wandering of his people in the desert. If we only take these writings literally as stories, then the Torah will have no impact on us.

But if we delve deeper, and understand what is truly described there, then the Five Books become a Kabbalistic revelation, wherein all the degrees of understanding of the spiritual worlds are expounded. This is exactly what Moses wanted to pass on.

The same relates to King Solomon's "Song of Songs." Everything depends on how it is read and perceived. Either just as a love song or as a spiritual revelation, on which the Zohar comments as the highest connection to the Creator.

It is important to find authentic Kabbalistic sources whose content will induce thoughts about the Creator and the goal that needs to be reached. Then there is no doubt you will reach it.

The sources that divert one from the true goal will not bring any good. The Surrounding Light, *Ohr Makif*, is drawn according to one's desire. The Light will not shine if one's desire does not aim at a genuine goal.

We speak of the number 600,000 souls; where does this originate? From a *Partzuf* made of 6 *Sefirot*, each one of them is in turn composed of 10. This *Partzuf* has risen to the level of 10,000. Hence the number 600,000.

We constantly breed different desires, whatever they are. Our development depends on the level of these desires.

In the beginning our desires are on the lowest level, the so-called animal desires. Later these are followed by desires for wealth, honor, social position and so on.

On a higher level are the desires for knowledge, music, art, culture, etc. Finally, we find the more elevated desire for spirituality.

Such desires gradually appear in the souls after many incarnations in this world or, as we say, with the development of generations.

First the souls living exclusively in their animal nature life were incarnated in our world. Then, next generations of souls experienced the desire for money, honor and power. Finally, these gave way to the desire for sciences and for something higher that the sciences cannot provide.

It is impossible for man to experience two different desires because this would mean that they have not been properly defined.

After they are carefully analyzed and sorted, it appears to be the one and only desire. A man receives several desires simultaneously. He then selects only one of them if he is able to correctly assess his level.

The spiritual Vessel (*Kli*) broke into 600,000 parts and lost its Screen. Now the Screen is to be rebuilt and the broken parts themselves must perform this task, so that they can "live" the path of return, feel what they are and create the Creator out of themselves.

The spiritual Vessel consists of two parts: one kind ranges from *Peh* down to *Tabur* and is called *Kelim de Ashpa'a* (Vessels of bestowing); they correspond to the desires to give without restraint.

Even though they are internally selfish, they operate according to the principle of giving without restraint.

The second part ranges from *Tabur* down and it is composed of purely selfish desires which operate for receiving, not giving, and they are called *Kelim de Kabbalah* (Vessels of Receiving).

The point of the matter is not that the upper desires are good, and the lower desires bad, but that the upper desires are "small," and the lower desires "big."

For this reason there is a Screen on the upper desires as opposed to the lower ones. The upper part of the *Partzuf* is called *Galgalta ve Eynaim*, the lower part is called *AHP*.

The weaker desires undergo their correction first; they do not require much time for this process. Then the desires under *Tabur* are corrected, these are more selfish.

The altruistic desires called *Galgalta ve Eynaim* need to be corrected first and next the egoistic desires called *AHP*. At the end of this process everything merges back into one common *Kli*. That is why the difference between the altruistic Vessels and the egoistic all comes down to the timing of correction.

The time for *Galgalta ve Eynaim*'s correction has come and their desires are exposed. They have reached a higher degree of development.

On the other hand, the *AHP* cannot proceed to the correction of their desires as these are still hidden in a latent state.

But when the time comes, we will realize how much bigger are the *AHPs'* desires compared to *Galgalta ve Eynaim*'s. As soon as these souls begin their correction, the already corrected souls of *Galgalta ve Eynaim* will be able to rise thanks to them.

The egoistic *Kelim*, the *AHP*, by virtue of their forthcoming correction, place high demands on *Galgalta ve Eynaim*, the altruistic *Kelim*. Many of the latter have not yet started their correction and obstruct the correction of the former.

In order to reach the spiritual world, our generation needs to read very specific literature.

Today it is the *Talmud Esser HaSefirot*. 500 years ago, it was books written by the Ari, Rabbi Isaac Luria. Before the Ari it was the Book of Zohar.

Each generation is offered a special book serving as a key to enter the spiritual world. This book corresponds to the development of the souls of the given generation.

Once a person actually reaches the spiritual world, he may read all the books because he now sees that each one of them is suitable for him.

Matching the spiritual world, achieving its attributes, means observing internally all its laws. As a consequence, the soul evolves.

When the time of complete attainment comes: all worlds—spiritual and material—will merge into a single whole. Man will then be able to live in all worlds at the same time.

Lesson 4

Topics examined in this lesson:

Lesson 4

Having journeyed thus far toward the goal of learning Kabbalah, we urge the student not to fall by the wayside due to difficulties with some of the technical nature of our explanations.

Through an earnest desire for true knowledge of the wisdom of Kabbalah, the student will be assisted from above through an awakening of the *Ohr Makif* (Surrounding Light).

When the time is right, the student will further his studies under the guidance of a qualified teacher as part of a group.

The important aspect is to bear in mind the level man needs to attain in order to give completely and not to receive anything for himself.

Then the person has reached completion, with a true *deveikut* (attachment). This is the goal of creation, and man was created just for this.

To return to our narrative: We wrote concerning the Light entering and leaving the *Partzuf*. Here we are discussing a fulfilled and unfulfilled desire.

When the Light enters the *Partzuf* this corresponds to the fulfillment of a desire, to a feeling of wholeness and delight.

When the Light leaves the *Partzuf* there remains a void or frustration. This happens in spite of the fact that there is no such thing as a feeling of void in the spiritual world.

If the *Ohr Hochma* exits, the *Ohr Hassadim* remains. Each time the *Partzuf* pushes the Light away, it knowingly understands where it is heading by refusing a certain amount of pleasure.

In the spiritual context, a selfish enjoyment is willingly refused and replaced by altruistic enjoyment in nature, which is much higher and stronger.

If the *Partzuf* perceives that it is unable to receive so as to please the Master, it will refuse to receive for itself.

It goes without saying that in order to make such a decision, some help, as well as a force opposing selfishness are required. This decisive role is played by the Screen (*Masach*).

With a Screen, the *Kli* (Vessel) begins to perceive the Light instead of darkness. The quantity of Light which is revealed is proportional to the strength of the Screen. Without a Screen, the Light does not allow any altruistic action. It is precisely the absence of Light during the First Restriction, operated by the *Kli*, which enables it to build a Screen.

By this means, it can allow the Light to enter. A desire can be considered spiritual only when the Screen is duly positioned.

We have previously studied the five *Partzufim* of the World of *Adam Kadmon*. As already outlined, the main task for a student of Kabbalah is to attain the Light, that is to say, the filling of the *Partzuf*, the soul, by the Light.

As soon as the Light enters the *Kli*, it immediately starts acting upon it and transmits to the *Kli* its own altruistic attributes, i.e., the ability to give.

Man then realizes what he is in comparison to the Light and begins to feel ashamed of receiving it; this makes him wish to resemble the Light.

The strength of the Divine Light cannot modify the nature of the *Kli* the Creator Himself has created; it can only change the orientation of its utilization: from self-aimed pleasure into pleasure for the sake of the Creator.

Such a scheme of utilizing the *Kli* is called "receiving for the sake of giving." It allows *Malchut* to completely enjoy receiving the Light, while returning this delight to the Creator. It then continues to enjoy, sharing now the Creator's delight.

During the first phase (*Behina Alef*) of the progression of the Straight Light (*Ohr Yashar*), *Malchut* only received pleasure from the Light that filled it.

However, because of the path followed by the Light all the way down from the World Without End (*Olam Ein Sof*) to our world, and conversely all the way back to the World Without End, but this time using a Screen, *Malchut* again fills up with all the Light, but with an intention turned toward the Creator. This makes it reach an endless delight.

Thanks to this process, all its desires, both the lowest and the highest, lead to never-ending delight. This is also designated by the expression "feeling of completeness and unity."

The five *Partzufim* of the World of *Adam Kadmon* have used all the *Reshimot* (Records) of the World of *Ein Sof*, by which it was possible to fill *Malchut* up to the *Tabur*.

Of course there still remain very powerful desires below the *Tabur* of *Galgalta*.

These desires are not endowed with a Screen and therefore cannot be filled with the Light. If we succeeded in filling up the lower part of *Galgalta* with the Light, the *Gmar Tikkun* (the Final Correction) would take place.

In order to complete this task, a new *Partzuf*, the *Nekudot de SAG*, which comes out while the Light is exiting the *Partzuf* of *SAG*, descends below the *Tabur* of *Galgalta*

We know that Galgalta bears the name of *Keter*, *AB* the name of *Hochma*, *SAG*: *Bina*, *MA*: *Zeir Anpin*, *BON*: *Malchut*.

The *Partzuf* of *Bina* is a *Partzuf* which may spread in every place. It has only the desire to give, it does not need any *Ohr Hochma*; its attribute is to give without restraint, *Ohr Hassadim*.

SAG was born on the *Reshimot* of *Gimel de Hitlabshut-Bet de Aviut*. Neither *Galgalta* nor *AB*, which work with selfish desires to receive, can descend below the *Tabur*, as they know that much stronger desires exist there.

Below the *Tabur* the *Nekudot de SAG* fill *Galgalta* with the Light of *Hassadim*, i.e. with the pleasures of giving. These pleasures can then be diffused without restraint to any desire in the *Partzuf*.

Below the Tabur, the *Nekudot de SAG* form a new Partzuf which contains its own 10 Sefirot: Keter, Hochma, Bina, Hesed, Gevura, Tifferet, Netzah, Hod, Yesod and Malchut.

This *Partzuf* bears the name of "*Nekudot de SAG*." It is of paramount importance in the whole process of correction, as being a part of *Bina*, which elevates the uncorrected desires to its level, corrects and rises above her.

From the top to the *Tabur*, *Galgalta* comprises:

(i) At the Head level: the *Sefirot* Keter, *Hochma* and *Bina*.

(ii) At the *Toch* level: *Hesed*, *Gevura* and *Tifferet*.

(iii) Below the *Tabur*, in the *Sof*: *Netzah*, *Hod*, *Yesod* and *Malchut*.

When the *Nekudot de SAG* descend below the *Tabur* and begin to transmit the Light of *Hassadim* to the *Sof* of *Galgalta*, they are subjected to a strong reaction on the part of the *Reshimot* remaining in the *Sof* of *Galgalta* from the Light that previously filled these *Kelim*.

These *Reshimot* are of strength *Dalet-Gimel*. The strength of the *Dalet-Gimel* (*Hitlabshut* of Level 4, *Aviut* of Level 3) is higher than the strength of the *Masach* of the *Nekudot de SAG* (*Hitlabshut* of Level 2, *Aviut* of Level 2). Therefore *SAG* cannot oppose such a powerful Light-Desire and begins to desire to receive it for itself.

We can now examine the *Bina* phase in the spreading of the Straight Light from above downward (See Figure 1).

This phase is composed of two parts:

(i) In the first it does not want to receive anything, while giving without restraint. This part is called *Gar de Bina* and is endowed with altruistic attributes.

(ii) The second part already considers receiving the Light, though in order to transmit it further on. Although it is receiving, it does not do it for its own sake. This part of *Bina* is called *Zat de Bina*.

The same thing occurs in the *Partzuf* of the *Nekudot de SAG*, which possesses the attributes of *Bina*:

The first six *Sefirot* bear the name of *Gar de Bina* and the last four *Sefirot* are named *Zat de Bina*. The powerful Light of *Hochma* that reaches *Gar de Bina* does not affect it; it is indifferent to this Light.

However, *Zat de Bina*, which desires to receive in order to give to the lower levels, may receive only that Light which relates to *Aviut Bet*.

If the desires reaching *Zat de Bina* are of a stronger *Aviut*, the desire to receive for oneself alone appears.

However, after the *Tzimtzum Alef* (First Restriction), *Malchut* cannot receive with a self-aimed intention.

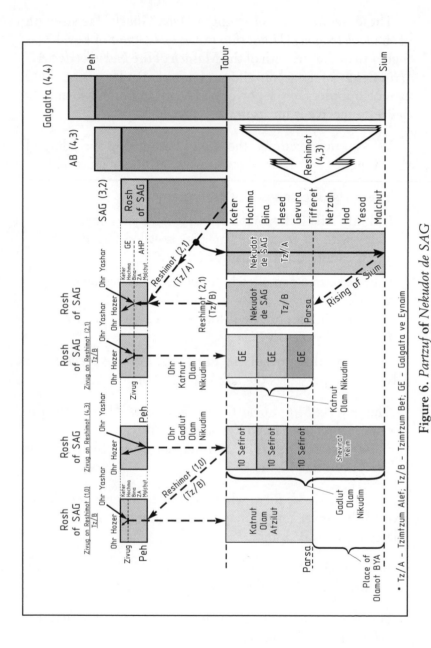

Figure 6. *Partzuf of Nekudot de SAG*

* Tz/A – Tzimtzum Alef; Tz/B – Tzimtzum Bet; GE – Galgalta ve Eynaim

Therefore, as soon as such a desire appears in the *Zat* of the *Nekudot de SAG*, *Malchut* rises and positions itself on the border between altruistic and selfish desires that is in the middle of *Tifferet*.

This act of *Malchut* is called *Tzimtzum Bet*, the second restriction. A new border for the spreading of the Light is being formed along this line: the *Parsa*. This border was located before in the *Sium* of *Galgalta*.

While the Light was previously able to spread only up to the *Tabur*, even though it tried to penetrate under it, with the spreading of the *Partzuf* of the *Nekudot de SAG* below the *Tabur*, the Light of *Hassadim* did penetrate there, and paved the way so to speak for the spreading of the Light of *Hochma* to the *Parsa*.

However, if before the *Tzimtzum Bet* the *Ohr Hassadim* could spread below the *Tabur*, afterward there would remain absolutely no Light below the *Parsa*.

The *Partzuf* of the *Nekudot de SAG* has created the concept of "place" (*Makom*) below the *Tabur*. What is a "place"? It is a *Sefira* inside of which another *Sefira*, smaller in dimension, can be fitted.

Our world exists in a "place." If one removes from the universe absolutely everything it contains, then the "place" will remain.

Man's finite mind cannot perceive it, but it can only be said that this is simply a void that cannot be measured since it is located in other dimensions.

In addition to our world there exist spiritual worlds that are impossible to perceive or feel because they refer to other dimensions.

Afterward, the World of *Atzilut* appears at the place of *Gar de Bina* below the *Tabur*. The World of *Beria* is formed under the *Parsa* in the lower section of *Tifferet*.

The World of *Yetzira* appears at the place of the *Sefirot Netzah, Hod, Yesod.* The World of *Assiya* whose last portion is called our world, is formed at the place of the *Sefira Malchut.*

How can 10 *Sefirot* be obtained out of 5: *Keter, Hochma, Bina, Zeir Anpin* and *Malchut?* Each of these *Sefirot*, with the exception of *Zeir Anpin*, is made up of 10 *Sefirot.*

Zeir Anpin, being a small entity, comprises six *Sefirot* only: *Hesed, Gevura, Tifferet, Netzah, Hod, Yesod.* If instead of *Zeir Anpin*, one places its six *Sefirot*, then along with *Keter, Hochma, Bina* and *Malchut*, 10 *Sefirot* will be obtained.

This is the reason why sometimes 5 or 10 *Sefirot* are mentioned. There is on the other hand, no such thing as a *Partzuf* with 12 or 9 *Sefirot.*

Lesson 5

Topics examined in this lesson:

Lesson 5

We shall commence with a brief review: the Creation is brought forth by the Light emanating from the Creator, and this Light is the desire to give delight, and is called *Behina Shoresh* (Root Phase).

It builds for itself the desire to receive delight, *Behina Alef*, which after being filled with the Light, adopts the attribute of the Light; that is the desire to give, to relentlessly bring delight. This corresponds to *Behina Bet*.

But there is nothing it has to give. It realizes that it can bring Him delight only if it accepts a portion of the Light for His sake.

So the third stage: *Zeir Anpin* is created. It already has two properties: to give and to receive.

After perceiving these two kinds of delight, *Zeir Anpin* feels that receiving is better and nicer than giving. This is its initial character in stage *Alef*.

Therefore it decides to receive all the Light and is completely filled with the Light, but now upon its own wish. Its delight is infinite.

This has become the fourth phase, called *Malchut* of the World of *Ein Sof*, the one and only true Creation. It combines the two conditions: it knows in advance what it wishes, and out of the two states it chooses receiving.

The first three phases do not bear the name of "Creation" because they do not possess a desire of their own, but only the Creator's or a consequence of it.

The fourth stage, after being filled with Light just as during the first phase, starts adopting the attributes of the Creator, and senses itself as a receiver.

A feeling of shame arises leading to the decision to become like the Creator, i.e. not to allow any Light in and the *Tzimtzum Alef* (First Restriction) takes place.

How is it that the *Tzimtzum* did not take place in the end of Phase 1? The answer is that during the first phase, the desire of the *Kli* was not its own, but was the wish of the Creator.

Here the creation restricts its own desire to receive, and does not use it.

Tzimtzum is made not on the desire to receive delight, but on the aspiration to receive for itself. It refers only to intention.

In the first case the *Kli* simply ceased to receive. Now, if the *Kli* made a decision to receive, but not for its own sake, it could fill itself with a certain portion of the Light, depending on the strength of its intention to counteract the force of egoism.

This reception of Light for the benefit of another is equal to bestowal. An action in the spiritual world is defined by its intention, not by the action itself.

The First Restriction means that the *Kli* will never use delight for its own sake. *Tzimtzum Alef* will never be violated.

That is why the primary task of a created being is the necessity to neutralize the wish to receive delight for its own sake.

The first created being, *Behina Dalet*, shows how to receive pleasure from all the Light of the Creator, although the First Restriction means that all that *Malchut* is filled up with will never be received as delight for its own sake.

We shall see how this principle can be further implemented.

Initially, *Malchut* places a Screen above its egoism, which pushes away all the incoming Light. This is a kind of test to check whether *Malchut* is able to resist all the enormous delight which presses against the Screen and which corresponds to an equally enormous desire to receive it.

Yes, it does succeed in pushing away all the delight, and does not luxuriate in it.

But in this case the *Kli* is separated from the Light. How does *Malchut* achieve a situation, when the delight is not simply pushed away, but some portion of it is received for the sake of the Creator?

For this to take place, the Light reflected by the Screen (*Ohr Hozer*) must somehow clothe the Straight Light (*Ohr Yashar*), and together they will enter the *Kli*, that is, the desire to receive.

Thus *Ohr Hozer* serves as the anti-egoistic condition, accepting and allowing in the *Ohr Yashar*, the delight.

Here *Ohr Hozer* acts as an altruistic intention. Before taking in these two kinds of Lights, a calculation is carried out in the *Rosh*. How much Light may be received for the Creator's sake? This quantity passes in the *Toch*.

The first *Partzuf* may receive, for example, twenty percent of the Light, according to the power of its Screen. This Light is called Inner Light—*Ohr Pnimi*.

The portion of Light which did not enter the *Kli*, remains outside and is therefore called the Surrounding Light, *Ohr Makif*.

The initial receiving of twenty percent of the Light is called *Partzuf Galgalta*.

Following the pressure of the two Lights, *Ohr Makif* and *Ohr Pnimi* on the Screen in the *Tabur*, the *Partzuf* expels all the Light. The Screen then moves gradually up from *Tabur* to *Peh*, losing its anti-egoistic power and reaching the level of the Screen in the *Peh de Rosh*.

Note that nothing disappears in the spiritual world, each consecutive action encompasses the previous one. Thus, the twenty percent of Light received from *Peh* to *Tabur* remains in the previous state of the *Partzuf*.

Afterwards, the *Partzuf*, seeing that it is not able to manage the 20% of Light, makes a decision to take the Light in again, this time not 20%, but 15%.

For this purpose, it has to lower its Screen from the level of *Peh* to the level of *Chazeh* of the *Partzuf Galgalta*, that is, to move down to a lower spiritual level.

If at the beginning its level was defined by the *Reshimot*: *Hitlabshut* of Level 4 and *Aviut* of Level 4, now it is only 4 and 3 respectively.

The Light enters the same way and forms a new *Partzuf*: *AB*. The destiny of the new *Partzuf* is the same; it also pushes the Light away.

Following on this occurrence, the third *Partzuf*, *SAG*, spreads out, and after it, *MA* and *BON*.

All five *Partzufim* fill *Galgalta* from its *Peh* to *Tabur*. The world which they form is called *Adam Kadmon*.

Galgalta is similar to the *Behina Shoresh*, since while receiving from the Creator it gives whatever it can.

AB receives a smaller portion for the sake of the Creator, and is called *Hochma*, as *Behina Alef*.

SAG works only for bestowal and is called *Bina*, as *Behina Bet*. *MA* is similar to *Zeir Anpin*, as *Behina Gimel*, and *BON* corresponds to *Malchut*, *Behina Dalet*.

SAG, having the properties of *Bina*, is able to spread under the *Tabur* and fill the lower part of *Galgalta* with the Light.

Below the *Tabur*, with the exception of empty desires, remain the delights induced by similarity with the Creator.

All this because the *NHY* (*Sefirot: Netzah Hod Yesod*) of *Galgalta* below the *Tabur* refused to take in the Light of *Hochma*. They enjoy the Light of *Hassadim*, the delight of similarity with the Creator. This delight is also on the level *Dalet de Aviut*.

The *Nekudot de SAG* have *Aviut Bet*, and may enjoy from bestowal of the Light on this level only. Hence they cannot longer resist the delight of the level *Dalet*, otherwise they will begin to receive the Light for their own sake.

The above should normally occur, but *Malchut* standing in the *Sium* of *Galgalta* rises to the middle of *Tifferet* of *Partzuf Nekudot de SAG* and forms a new *Sium* (Conclusion). This is the restriction of the Light, called *Parsa*, below which the Light cannot go.

With this action *Malchut* makes the second restriction on the spreading of the Light, called *Tzimtzum Bet* by analogy with the first one.

To take an example from our everyday life: imagine a man with pleasant manners and good upbringing who would never steal up to the sum of $1000. However, if $10,000 were laid before him, his education might not "work" because in this case, the temptation, the prospective delight, is too powerful to be resisted.

Tzimtzum Bet is the continuation of *Tzimtzum Alef*, but on the Vessels of receiving, the *Kelim de Kabbalah*.

It is interesting to note that in the *Nekudot de SAG*, the *Partzuf*, which is altruistic by nature, has disclosed its selfish properties; immediately *Malchut*, ascending upward, covers it and forms a line, called *Parsa*, to limit the downward spreading of the Light.

The *Rosh* of the *Partzuf SAG*, as every Head, consists of five *Sefirot*: *Keter*, *Hochma*, *Bina*, *Zeir Anpin* and *Malchut*. These in turn, are divided into the *Kelim de Ashpa'a* (*Keter*, *Hochma* and half of *Bina*) and *Kelim de Kabbalah* (from the middle of *Bina* to *Malchut*).

Kelim de Ashpa'a (Vessels of bestowal) are also called *Galgalta ve Eynaim*.

The Kelim de Kabbalah are the Awzen, Hotem, Peh: AHP.

The restriction of *Tzimtzum Bet* means that from this point on a *Partzuf* must not activate any of the Vessels of receiving. It is prohibited to use *AHP*; so decided *Malchut*, when it rose to the middle of *Tifferet*.

After *Tzimtzum Bet* all the *Reshimot* move up to the *Rosh* of SAG, there requesting to form a *Partzuf* of the level of *Galgalta ve Eynaim* exclusively. This allows the *Partzuf* to receive some Light from contact with the Creator.

It now means that the Screen must be located not in *Peh de Rosh*, but in *Nikveh Eynaim*, which corresponds to the line of *Parsa* in the middle of *Tifferet* in *Guf*.

After a *Zivug* in *Rosh* of SAG, a *Partzuf* will emerge from this point and will spread below the *Tabur* and down to the *Parsa*.

The new *Partzuf*, which spreads below the *Tabur* to *Parsa*, clothes the previous *Partzuf* of *Nekudot de SAG*, but on its upper part only, meaning on altruistic *Kelim*.

The name of the new *Partzuf* is *Katnut* of *Olam Nikudim* (Smallness of the World of *Nikudim*). This *Partzuf* appears on the level of the restricted *Reshimot* of *Bet-Alef*.

In fact, of the five worlds previously mentioned (*Adam Kadmon, Atzilut, Beria, Yetzira* and *Assiya*) there does not exist such a world, because as soon as it was born, it broke apart immediately.

During the brief existence of this world, the *Sefirot* of *Keter, Hochma, Bina, Hesed, Gevura* and the one third of *Tifferet* are divided into ten and have the usual names.

In addition, there are special names for the *Sefirot* of *Hochma* and *Bina*: *Abba ve Ima* (Father and Mother) and also, the *Sefirot* of *Zeir Anpin* and *Malchut*: ZON, *Zeir Anpin* and *Nukva* (Female).

Following the *Zivug de Aka'a* in the *Nikveh Eynaim* in *Rosh* of *SAG*, upon the request of the *Reshimot* of the lower *Partzuf*, SAG performs a second *Zivug* on the *Reshimot* of *Gadlut* (Greatness) in the *Peh de Rosh*.

As this action takes place, a great Light begins to spread out from *SAG* and tries to descend below the *Parsa*.

Partzuf of *Nikudim* is absolutely certain that it will be able to receive the Light for the sake of the Creator, and that it has enough power for this, notwithstanding the *Tzimtzum Bet*.

However, at the moment the Light touches the *Parsa*, the *Shevirat haKelim* (Shattering of the Vessels) occurs, because it becomes clear that the *Partzuf* wants to receive delight for itself only. Light immediately exits the *Partzuf* and all the *Kelim*, even those which were above the *Parsa*, are shattered.

So from the desire of the *Partzuf* to use the *Kelim de Kabbalah* for the Creator's sake; to form the World of *Nikudim in Gadlut*, using all ten *Kelim*, a shattering of all its screen-intentions occurred.

In the *Guf* of the *Partzuf Nikudim*, i.e. in *ZON* above the *Parsa* (*Hesed*, *Gevura*, *Tifferet*) and below the *Parsa* (*Netzah*, *Hod*, *Yesod* and *Malchut*) there are eight *Sefirot*. Each of these consists of four phases (apart from phase zero).

These, in turn, bear ten *Sefirot*, yielding a total of 320 *Kelim* (4 x 8 x 10), which have been broken.

Of the 320 broken *Kelim*, only *Malchut* cannot be corrected and this represents 32 parts (4 x 8).

The remaining 288 parts (320 — 32) can be corrected. The 32 parts are called *Lev haEven* (lit. Heart of Stone). These will only be corrected by the Creator Himself at the time of *Gmar Tikkun* (Final Correction).

The altruistic and selfish desires have simultaneously broken apart and intermingled. As a result, every element of the broken *Kelim* consists of 288 parts that are fit for correction and 32 which are not.

Now the achievement of the goal of Creation only depends on the correction of the broken World of *Nikudim*. If we succeed in our required task, the *Behina Dalet* will be filled with the Light.

Olam haTikkun (World of Correction) is created to build a coherent system which will then correct the *Kelim* of the World of *Nikudim*.

This new world is also called *Olam Atzilut* (World of Emanation).

Lesson 6

Topics examined in this lesson:

1. 125 Levels
2. The Sin of Adam HaRishon
3. The Shattering of the Vessels
4. The Breaking of the Souls
5. The Breaking of the Worlds
6. World of *Nikudim*
7. World of Correction
8. *Partzufim* of World of *Atzilut*
9. The birth of the Worlds of *BYA*

Lesson 6

There are five worlds between the Creator and our world. Each of them consists of five *Partzufim* and each *Partzuf* of five *Sefirot*.

In total there are 125 levels between us and the Creator. *Malchut*, moving through all these levels, reaches the last one, and in this way, *Behina Dalet*, the only creation, merges with the four previous phases.

Malchut fully absorbs the properties of the four phases and thus becomes equal to the Creator. This is the Goal of Creation.

In order to mix *Malchut* with the remaining nine *Sefirot*, a special *Partzuf* is created. This consists of *Malchut* and the nine *Sefirot* from *Keter* to *Yesod*. Its name is *Adam*.

In the beginning, the nine *Sefirot* and the tenth, *Malchut*, are not connected to each other in any way. That's why it was said that in the beginning Adam was forbidden to eat the fruit of the Tree of the Knowledge of Good and Evil.

With the fall of Adam and the shattering of his *Kelim*, the four upper phases, or the nine first *Sefirot*, fall into *Malchut*. Here the fourth stage can choose to remain the same old *Malchut* or to prefer spiritual development in the similarity of the four phases.

If *Malchut* remains like its own self, this means that *Malchut*, or the soul, or Adam, is in the World of *Assiya*, though, if it becomes like the third phase, then *Malchut* is in the World of *Yetzira*.

The similarity to the second phase means that *Malchut* is in the World of *Beria*. Similarity to the first stage corresponds to *Malchut* in the World of *Atzilut*. Finally, similarity to the zero phase means existence of *Malchut* in the World of *Adam Kadmon*.

All spiritual movements from above downward, from *Malchut of the Ein Sof* to our world, and back to the World of *Ein Sof*, are preordained.

Nothing is planned that is not in accordance with the goal of Creation. This goal is achieved when the fourth stage becomes similar to the third, second, first and zero stages, which are all contained in the fourth stage.

All the worlds appear as the descent of the Creator from above downward, over the 125 levels of the five worlds. This is like a permanent restriction of the Creator, making the whole of Creation recede from Him until Creation reaches the level of our world, which no longer feels Him.

When Creation rises upward, it makes its way through the same 125 levels of the five worlds, which were formed for this specific purpose. Advancing a single level provides you with the power to take a leap forward to the next one.

The descent from above to below is the regression process of the soul, but the ascent is progression.

During the descent, the power of each level lessens, because it conceals more and more of the Light of the Creator from His Creation. But the reverse movement increasingly reveals to man the Light of the Creator and consequently grants him the power to overcome obstacles.

Let us explain what happens when *Shevirat haKelim* takes place.

The nine altruistic *Sefirot* that *Malchut*, being the selfish part, tries to use for its own sake, fall into *Malchut*. At this time, altruism and selfishness are blended together.

Now, if a strong Light enlightens this blend and awakens *Malchut*, making it understand its own nature and what the Creator is, this enables *Malchut* to strive to be like the upper *Sefirot*, i.e. the Light of the Creator.

Even though *Shevirat haKelim* is, so to say, an anti-spiritual action, actually it is the only possible process that can enable *Malchut* to bond with the altruistic properties of the Creator and to rise up to His level at a later stage.

After *Shevirat haKelim*, two parallel systems of worlds, *Assiya, Yetzira, Beria, Atzilut* and *Adam Kadmon* are built as two systems: altruistic and selfish. These worlds are built on the basis of *Shevirat haKelim*, which is why their system specifically grasps a man's soul.

The soul of man also consists of selfish and altruistic *Kelim*. The Fall of Adam combined these two sorts of *Kelim* and his *Partzuf* was broken.

When ascending to the appropriate level in the system of worlds, each such broken part may discover its respective attribute there.

Shevirat Neshamot (the breaking of souls) of Adam and *Shevirat Nikudim* are built on the same basis. The worlds are a kind of outer casing for the soul.

In our material world, it is the Universe, the Earth and everything around us, which forms the outer casing, enclosing mankind within it.

When examining how the World of *Atzilut* is designed, we may note that its structure completely matches the World of *Nikudim*. The *Nekudot de SAG*, after *Tzimtzum Bet*, ascend to the *Rosh* of *SAG* with three kinds of *Reshimot*.

From the restricted *Reshimot* of *Bet-Alef*, the World of *Nikudim* is formed in the *Katnut* on *Kelim Galgalta ve Eynaim*. This spreads downward from the *Tabur* to *Parsa*.

This *Partzuf*, like any other, is composed of *Rosh* and *Guf*. Its *Rosh* is divided into three parts: the first division of the *Rosh* is called *Rosh Keter*, the second *Rosh Abba* (*Hochma*) and the third *Rosh Ima* (*Bina*).

The *Guf* of the World of *Nikudim* is called ZON—*Zeir Anpin* and *Nukva*. Above the *Parsa* is *Gar de* ZON, below the *Parsa* we find *Zat de* ZON.

Following this the World of *Nikudim* craved to enter the *Gadlut*, i.e., to join the *AHPs* to itself. But when the upper Light reached *Parsa* and tried to cross it, the World of *Nikudim* broke apart.

Rosh Keter and *Rosh Abba ve Ima* remain, since the Heads do not break.

But ZON, i.e., *Guf*, breaks completely, both above the *Parsa*, and below it. Now, there are in total 320 broken parts, 32 of which (*Lev haEven*) are not possible to correct by one's own power. The remaining 288 parts are subject to correction.

Next, in order to correct the broken *Kelim*, *Olam haTikkun* (*Olam Atzilut*) is created. *Reshimot* from the breakage of all 320 parts ascend to *Rosh* of *SAG*.

At the beginning, the *Rosh* of *SAG* selects the purest parts, the lightest with respect to the ability to be corrected.

This is the law of correction: first the easiest parts get corrected and then with their help, the next parts are handled.

Out of the corrected *Kelim*, *Rosh* of *SAG* creates the *Partzufim* of the World of *Atzilut*, similar to a small World of *Nikudim*:

(i) *Keter* of the World of *Atzilut*, also named *Atik*

(ii) *Hochma*, also named *Arich Anpin*

(iii) *Bina*, also named *Abba ve Ima*

(iv) *Zeir Anpin*

(v) *Nukva*, also named *Malchut*

The World of *Atzilut* is a replica of the World of *Nikudim*. *Atik* is between the *Tabur* of *Galgalta* and *Parsa, Arich Anpin* from *Peh* of *Atik* to *Parsa, Abba ve Ima* from *Peh* of *Arich Anpin* to *Tabur* of *Arich Anpin*. *Zeir Anpin* stands from *Tabur* of *Arich Anpin* to *Parsa, Malchut* is in the form of a point under *Zeir Anpin* (see Figure 7).

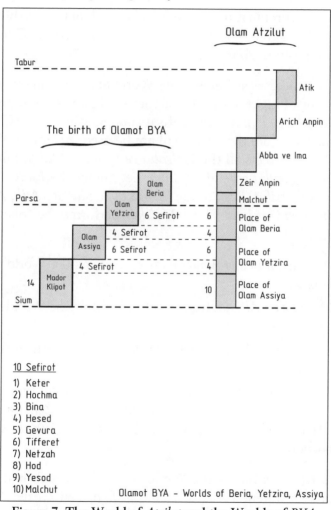

Figure 7. The World of *Atzilut* and the Worlds of *BYA*

Each *Partzuf* is composed of two parts: *Galgalta ve Eynaim*, *Kelim* of bestowal, and *AHPs*, *Kelim* of reception.

After being shattered, the Vessel consists not of two parts, but of four: *Galgalta ve Eynaim*, *AHP*, *Galgalta ve Eynaim* inside *AHP* and *AHP* inside *Galgalta ve Eynaim*.

Such a combination can be found in each of the 320 broken *Kelim*. The aim is to break each particle and separate *Galgalta ve Eynaim* from *AHP*.

The process is as follows: the World of *Atzilut* directs a ray of powerful Light to every non-corrected part, separating out its *Galgalta ve Eynaim*, then lifts it and sets aside the *AHP*, the *Kelim*. Therefore the *AHPs* will not be used. After the World of *Atzilut* corrects all the *Galgalta ve Eynaim*, *Malchut* of the World of *Atzilut* ascends to *Bina*, i.e., under the *Rosh* of the World of *Atzilut*. *Rosh* of the World of *Atzilut* are *Atik*, *Arich Anpin*, *Abba ve Ima*. There *Malchut* performs the following actions:

(i) *Zivug* on *Bet de Aviut* (level 2), creating the World of *Beria*.

(ii) *Zivug* on *Alef de Aviut* (level 1), creating the World of *Yetzira*.

(iii) *Zivug* in *Aviut Shoresh* (level 0), giving birth to the World of *Assiya*.

The ascent of *Bina* moves the World of *Atzilut* two levels up: *Malchut* is now in the place of *Abba ve Ima*, *Zeir Anpin* in the place of *Arich Anpin*, and *Arich Anpin* and *Atik* ascend in proportion.

Partzuf Malchut of the World of *Atzilut*, which is in this ascent equivalent to *Bina*, *Abba ve Ima*, can create, "give birth."

The result is that the World of *Beria* is born out of *Malchut* of *Atzilut* and occupies a new place instead of *Zeir Anpin* of the World of *Atzilut*, under the *Rosh*, that has given birth to it. The newborn is usually one level below its mother.

After this, the World of *Yetzira* is brought to life. Its first four *Sefirot*, i.e. its upper part, now occupies the place of *Malchut* of the World of *Atzilut*. Though in its lower part, six lower *Sefirot*, are located, correspondingly, in the position of the first six *Sefirot*, the place of the World of *Beria*.

The next world, *Assiya*, covers half of the World of *Beria* and half of the World of *Yetzira*. The four *Sefirot* of the World of *Yetzira* and ten *Sefirot* of the World of *Assiya* remain empty.

This empty place is called *Mador Klipot*, the place of evil forces.

In order to emphasize its importance we can consider the whole process once more:

The World of *Nikudim* went out in *Katnut* with *Rosh* being *Keter*, *Rosh* being *Abba ve Ima*, ZON being its *Guf*.

All this is called *Galgalta ve Eynaim* and spreads from *Tabur* to *Parsa*. After this the *Gadlut* of the World of *Nikudim* begins to emerge, which has ten *Sefirot* both in *Rosh* and *Guf*.

Gadlut appeared in *Keter*, in *Abba ve Ima*, but when ZON wants to receive *Gadlut* the World of *Nikudim* breaks apart.

All the *Kelim* of *Guf* break into 320 parts, they fall under *Parsa* and combine with each other, yielding four groups:

(i) *Galgalta ve Eynaim*

(ii) *AHP*

(iii) *Galgalta ve Eynaim* in *AHP*

(iv) *AHP* in *Galgalta ve Eynaim*

To correct the broken *Kelim*, the World of *Atzilut* is created. Firstly, its three *Partzufim* are born: *Atik, Arich Anpin, Abba ve Ima*, which fully correspond to the *Partzufim*: *Keter* and *Abba ve Ima* in the World of *Nikudim*.

Zeir Anpin and *Malchut* correspond to the same *Partzufim* in the World of *Nikudim*.

At this stage, the correction of the extracted *Kelim Galgalta ve Eynaim* from all the 320 parts is finished.

Further, we have *Galgalta ve Eynaim* inside the *AHP*s. There is no way to extract it, but the directed ray of Light may bring it closer to the Light.

Atzilut wants to do the correction in *AHP*. *Malchut* ascends to *Bina* and gives birth to the ten *Sefirot* of the World of *Beria*, which stands in place of *Zeir Anpin* of *Atzilut* because *Malchut* of the World of *Atzilut* is now in *Abba ve Ima*.

At this stage the ten *Sefirot* of the World of *Yetzira* are brought about; the last one partially overlaps the World of *Beria*. The part of the World of *Yetzira* is under *Parsa* in the place of the upper half of the World of *Beria*.

Finally, the World of *Assiya* is located from the middle part of the place of the World of *Beria* to the middle part of the place of the World of *Yetzira*.

Beginning in the middle of the place of the World of *Yetzira* and finally ending in the place of the World of *Assiya* is emptiness, *Mador Klipot*.

Presently we will see that the worlds can ascend and descend, but always moving together with respect to their initial position.

All that has been discussed in the present chapter is described in the 1500 pages of the *Talmud Esser HaSefirot* (Study of the 10 *Sefirot*) by Rabbi Yehuda Ashlag. This work of major importance provides guidelines for our spiritual progression and helps us to keep focused on the correct goal.

Our correction pertains to the Second Restriction, *Tzimtzum Bet*. As a result we cannot see beyond *Tzimtzum Alef*, the First Restriction. Actually, there is no human way to even imagine what sort of forces operate there, nor the nature of reality that exists in this place. These are referred to as the secrets of the Kabbalah.

Lesson 7

Topics examined in this lesson:

Lesson 7

The first *Partzuf* of the World of *Atzilut*, *Atik*, comes out on the *Reshimot* of *Alef-Shoresh* (*Hitlabshut* of Level 1, *Aviut* of Level 0) in the *Katnut* at first, from *Tabur* to *Parsa*. Then it spreads in the *Gadlut* all the way to our world on the *Reshimot* of *Dalet-Gimel* (4,3).

It is the only a *Partzuf* by means of which the Light can shine in our world. We do not see or feel this Light, but it shines and drives us forward.

Whoever ascends from our world to below *Parsa*, where the worlds *Beria*, *Yetzira* and *Assiya* are located, is called a righteous man, a *tzadik*.

It should be noted that the *Partzuf Atik* spreads not only to the *Parsa*, in order to pass on Light to other *Partzufim* of the World of *Atzilut*, but below the *Parsa* as well.

Since *Atik* is in *Tzimtzum Alef*, this *Partzuf* is able to spread everywhere, and when it is below the *Parsa* it lights up the souls of the righteous who want to ascend to the World of *Atzilut*.

Being in the Worlds of *BYA* means "giving for the sake of bestowal," while being in the World of *Atzilut* means "receiving for the sake of bestowal." The next *Partzuf*, *Arich Anpin*, *Hochma*, comes out in *Katnut*. After this *Partzuf*, *Abba ve Ima* (*Bina*) is born, then *Partzuf Zeir Anpin*, and finally *Malchut* is born in the form of a point.

The *AHP*s of the five *Partzufim* of the World of *Atzilut* are the *Kelim de Kabbalah*, Vessels for receiving. They are to be restored and corrected.

The World of *Atzilut* is the only world we study. All the others we study inasmuch as they are related to the World of *Atzilut*.

The aim is to ultimately raise all the souls to *Atzilut*. *Partzuf Arich Anpin* wraps itself up with many different coverings, which are called *Se'arot*, hair, similar to the hair of the human body.

The Light is passed onto all the lower worlds through the *Se'arot*. If the souls in the lower worlds desire the Light of *Hochma*, they apply to *Arich Anpin* and receive this Light through its "13 kinds of mercy"—13 parts of the *Partzuf* of *Se'arot*.

If this *Partzuf* contracts, the flowing of the Light ceases, and through this occurrence all the worlds suffer. All kinds of exiles stem from this.

But if *Arich Anpin* allows the Light to pass through it, such a period is considered very beneficial.

In order to receive the Light of *Hochma* from *Arich Anpin*, it is necessary to rise in its *Rosh*.

When *Malchut* of the World of *Atzilut* ascends to the level of *Arich Anpin*, it indicates that *Malchut* improves its properties to such an extent that it becomes similar to *Arich Anpin*.

This process unfolds as follows: first a request from *Malchut* is sent to *Abba ve Ima*, which performs a correction on *Malchut*, and then *Malchut* ascends to the *Rosh* of *Arich Anpin*.

There can only be the Light of *Hassadim* in the next *Partzuf*, *Abba ve Ima*. *Malchut* and *Zeir Anpin* are being corrected with the help of this Light, and further they are able to receive the Light of *Hochma* from the *Rosh* of *Arich Anpin*.

Abba ve Ima creates additional *Partzufim*, which enter *Zeir Anpin* and *Malchut*, in order to show by example how to carry out different actions.

Such an additional *Partzuf*, which gives power and knowledge to *Zeir Anpin* and *Malchut*, is called *Tzelem* (image or semblance).

Everything that corrects relates to *Abba ve Ima*. Everything that is corrected relates to *Malchut* and *Zeir Anpin*.

Why are only these two *Partzufim* to be corrected? Because these two *Partzufim* were broken in the World of *Nikudim*.

The first three *Partzufim* of the World of *Atzilut* came out on the *Reshimot* of *Rosh* (Heads) of the World of *Nikudim*.

Zeir Anpin of the World of *Atzilut* is called "Ha Kadosh Baruch Hu" (The Holy One Blessed Be He).

Malchut of the World of *Atzilut* is called *Shechina*—the aggregation of all the souls.

All the names, including the names of personages mentioned in the Bible, spring from the World of *Atzilut*. Those personages, furthermore, who are in the Worlds of *BYA*, all the same, are under the control of the World of *Atzilut*.

The World of *Atzilut* does not let through any Light below the *Parsa* apart from a tiny ray of Light, *Ohr Tolada*. This is done in order to avoid *Shevirat haKelim* (the shattering of the Vessels) again, as had happened in the World of *Nikudim*.

How are the *AHPs*, located below the *Parsa*, corrected? They are illuminated with a powerful Light by which they see how they differ from the Creator.

They then wish to improve themselves and apply to the Partzuf located above, which is the Creator for them. They ask for the feature of bestowal, or in other words a Masach

(Screen). If the request coming from AHP is authentic, the Partzuf located above lifts it out of the Worlds of BYA and into the World of Atzilut.

The filling with Light only takes place in the World of *Atzilut*. *AHPs* in the Worlds of *BYA* are actually seven *Sefirot* of *Zeir Anpin* and nine lower *Sefirot* of *Malchut* of the World of *Atzilut*; it is so because *Galgalta ve Eynaim* of *Zeir Anpin* and the *Sefira* of *Keter* of *Malchut* are in the World of *Atzilut*.

The request for help ascends to *AHPs* of *Zeir Anpin* and *Malchut*, located in the Worlds of *BYA*.

If these *Sefirot* can be lifted and attached to the corresponding *Sefirot* of the World of *Atzilut*, then it will be possible to fill them with Light. Such a condition is called *Gmar Tikkun* (Final Correction).

What is the difference between the ascending *AHPs* from those which are reached by the Light coming below the *Parsa*? The difference is qualitative: when *AHP* goes up, it is used as a Vessel for bestowal, not for receiving. Its main feature of receiving is removed during the ascension.

It is thus used as *Galgalta ve Eynaim*. This adds something to the World of *Atzilut*, but does not correct the *AHP* fundamentally. While ascending, *AHP* does not use its own Light but the Light of *Galgalta ve Eynaim*.

In addition to *AHPs* that can be raised to the World of *Atzilut*, there are many *Kelim* left in *BYA* that cannot be raised. This is because they are not combined with *Galgalta ve Eynaim*.

What is to be done in order to correct these *Kelim*? Just like the *Shevirat haKelim* in the worlds, a *Shevirat haKelim* in the souls is produced.

For this purpose *Malchut* of the *Ein Sof*—which is nothing more than a purely selfish created being, devoid of altruism and in a state of restriction that it accepted on itself—is added to the *Kelim* of *Galgalta ve Eynaim* of the ZON of the World of *Atzilut*.

Here there will be such a combination of *Kelim de Kabbalah* with *Kelim de Ashpa'a*, that naturally, such a *Partzuf* will break into smaller particles.

Further, the separate sparks of altruism and selfishness will combine, paving the way for the correction of *Malchut* by means of these same particles.

And so, after the World of *Atzilut* enters the state of *Katnut*, *Malchut* of the World of *Atzilut* ascends to the level of *Ima (Bina)* of the World of *Atzilut* and there gives birth to the World of *Beria*, by making a *Zivug* on the *Aviut Bet*.

After the second *Zivug* of *Malchut* on the *Aviut Gimel*, the World of *Yetzira* is born.

Then the World of *Assiya* is brought about after the third *Zivug* of *Malchut* on the *Aviut Dalet*.

After all this, a fundamentally new *Partzuf* is being created in *Katnut* with *Galgalta ve Eynaim*. The *AHP* of this new *Partzuf* in the future *Gadlut* will be *Malchut* of the *Ein Sof* itself.

This *Partzuf* is called *Adam HaRishon* (First Man). But why were these additional Worlds of *BYA* created? This is to build the necessary environment for this *Partzuf*, wherein it would exist and receive from all around the required Light, to match its ever changing desires.

As in the World of *Nikudim*, *Partzuf* of *Adam HaRishon* is born in *Katnut* with *Kelim* of *Galgalta ve Eynaim*.

Similar to all *Partzufim*, it wishes to enter to *Gadlut*. But the moment it starts to receive Light for *Gadlut*, in the *Kelim de Kabbalah* (*AHP*) of *Malchut* of the *Ein Sof*, it breaks up into small particles.

When Adam was born, he was absolutely righteous (a *tzadik*), he was already circumcised, and devoid of *Kelim de Kabbalah*.

Then, as he developed, he wanted to correct the whole Garden of Eden, i.e. all his desires.

This, in spite of strict instructions from the Creator, not to do *Zivug* on *Malchut* of *Malchut*, which is not able to absorb altruistic intentions, any *Kelim de Ashpa'a* that will fall into it.

Adam had no qualms about his capacity to perform a correction on *Malchut* of the *Ein Sof*, because it was his *AHP*.

But the moment Light began to descend from the World of *Atzilut* below the *Parsa*, *Adam HaRishon* was shattered into a great number of parts (600,000).

Each of these parts has to spend 6,000 years striving to accomplish its individual correction. The part of selfishness that a man may sacrifice to the Creator is called the soul.

In the instant of breaking up, all the desires of Adam fell down to the lowest level of selfishness. At this point all the fragments are separated, and each separate particle strives to draw pleasure and delight from this world.

This explains why special conditions were established to help man strengthen his bonding with the Creator and to receive the correcting Light from above.

While undergoing correction, a man sends a request to the Creator, for assistance to correct all his desires. The Light of the Creator comes down, and this man must undergo 6,000 consecutive actions to correct his soul.

When this happens, the soul becomes similar in its attributes to *Malchut* of the *Ein Sof*. It then receives all the Light for the sake of the Creator.

Everything we discover relates to the World of *Atzilut* and to the *Partzuf* of *Adam HaRishon*.

All that is written in the Kabbalah concerns some part of this *Partzuf*, or the world in which it comes out.

The perception of the surrounding world at any given time depends on how high a level man has risen to, and which part of the *Partzuf* of *Adam HaRishon*.

In order to bond with the spiritual world, a man has to achieve a similarity of attributes with this world.

If even only one desire matches the spiritual attribute of giving relentlessly, then at this stage, a connection with the Creator is established.

It is quite difficult to establish this first contact. When a man opens up to the spiritual he clearly comprehends it and cannot mistake it. He then needs to transform his desires. The Creator, for His part, wants man to achieve correction and expects man's request.

The Divine Light exists in an absolute stillness, only the souls are transformed. At every stage of the transformation they receive new information from the Light.

The Creator only replies to sincere prayer-desire. If there is no answer, it means that this is not yet a true desire to be answered.

When man is ready, the answer comes immediately, because the Light always wants to fill the *Kli*.

Lesson 8

Topics examined in this lesson:

Lesson 8

All sacred scriptures describe the feelings that a man is expected to live out. The message is always the same: that we are to prefer spirituality to the lures of the material world, and to praise the Creator.

The Creator does not stand in need of our praises, because He is totally devoid of egoism.

The only thing He wishes is to fill each one of us with delight. This is proportionate to our desire to choose Him amongst all other things, and to our aspirations to achieve attributes similar to His.

The glorification of the Creator is an indication of the correct orientation of the *Kli*. The delights from bonding with the Creator can become infinite, eternal, perfect and are only restricted by the intervening of a person's egoism.

Altruism is a specific attribute, a means of correcting the *Kli*. Egoism does not bring any good, worthwhile thing. It is plain to see: the more people have, the more likely they are not to be satisfied. The most developed countries often have an alarming rate of suicides amongst young and old.

One may give everything to a person; this often results in a lack of feeling for the simple tastes of life.

Taste is sensed only when suffering and pleasure come into contact. The fulfillment of a pleasure leads to the quenching of the desire to receive it.

The Creator's commandment to change the egoistic nature of the *Kli* into an altruistic one, is given for our benefit, not for His own sake.

The present condition of man is called *Olam Hazeh* (This World), but its next condition is *Olam Haba* (World to Come). A world is what one feels at a present moment, the next, elevated perceived feeling leads to the perception of a new world.

Each student, even if he attended a short course in Kabbalah and then walked away, would still receive something that would keep on living inside him.

Each one of us feels unconsciously what the most important thing in life is.

People are all different. Some were born smarter and are quicker. Such people often gain success in business and in society. They become wealthy and begin to exploit others.

Some people are born lazy, they grow and develop slowly, they are not very lucky. Some might even work harder than the smart ones, but get little in return.

We are not able to assess in this world the efforts of a person, as they depend on a great number of inner qualities that men are born with.

There are no devices that could measure the inner, moral efforts of a man, nor the physical ones.

The Baal HaSulam, Rabbi Y. Ashlag, writes that approximately ten percent of people in this world are so-called altruists. These are people who receive delight from giving.

Just as an egoist may kill for not receiving, such an "altruist" may kill for not being able to give. Giving is just a means of receiving delight for him.

Such people are, in a way, egoists as well, because their intention is to receive something as a result of their bestowal.

Naturally they also have to undergo correction. With regards to the spiritual they are all the same. They have to go a long way in order to grasp the inherent evil in their not being genuine altruists. This is the period in which they realize they are egoists.

The "coarser," the more egoistic a man is, the closer he is to seizing the opportunity to move on to spirituality. His egoism is as mature, as it is enormous.

Now, one further step is required, to realize that this egoism is evil to man himself. He must then plead with the Creator to change his intention from "receiving for one's sake" to "receiving for the sake of the Creator."

The attribute of shame appears in *Malchut* of the *Ein Sof*, when it realizes what *Keter, Behina Shoresh* is like. It is the sensation of the sharp contrast existing between the Light and itself.

Malchut itself does not perceive the Light, only the attributes and properties which are awakened in it by the Light.

Light itself does not possess any attributes. Those attributes that *Malchut* feels are the result of the influence that the Light has upon it.

All the reactions of the human organism are useful and necessary, whether we speak about the spiritual or material organism.

It is considered that all diseases are the reaction of the organism in order to maintain a state of balance.

Assume that a man has a fever. His organism produces a high temperature to kill germs, to protect itself. This reaction is always perceived not as an unhealthy condition of the organism, but as an outer manifestation, a reaction to an inner process.

That is why it is wrong to kill the symptoms of the diseases, i.e. to neutralize the reaction of the organism.

Our egoism is very clever. If there are any desires impossible to satisfy, it suppresses them in order not to bring needless suffering.

However, the moment certain conditions arise, these desires resurface.

The above is true for even a weak, ill or old person, who does not have any special desires except one: to remain alive. The organism suppresses the desires that are not to be fulfilled.

The evolution of the world is divided into the four stages of *Ohr Yashar*, when *Behina Alef* turned to *Bet*, *Bet* to *Gimel* and so on.

But when *Malchut* of the *Ein Sof* was formed, it absorbed all the desires of the upper *Sefirot*, which live in *Malchut* and do not change in any way.

The fact that other worlds were formed later on does not bear witness to changing desires, but to evolving intentions.

Depending on the intention, different desires are activated. But the desires themselves do not change. Nothing new that was not there previously is created.

It is the same with the thoughts that came to us today, but not yesterday. They were there before, but yesterday they were concealed from us.

Everything is in a latent state inside of man, and there is a time for the unfolding of each action. Nothing new is created.

It is impossible to transform two different things into one another. For example to change inorganic nature into organic, or beings of the vegetative kingdom into members of the animal one, etc.

The intermediate classes do exist, for example, halfway between the vegetative and animal worlds, i.e. the corals of the sea. Between vegetative and animal we may find a living organism feeding on the soil.

The ape is located halfway between the animal and human realm of existence. It cannot be a complete animal, but neither will it ever be a human being.

The only transformation that may occur is when a divine spark draws man to the spiritual and fosters the desire to attain, to reach for something higher.

At this stage then, this two-legged creature becomes a true man. There are only very few men that may be called "man" from the Kabbalistic point of view.

The development of science and technology is bound to reach an eventual deadlock and make us come to the conclusion that that is not the main goal. But first of all this state of deadlock needs to be reached.

Kabbalists have always organized groups of students. Under no circumstances are the students to be ranked or distinguished according to their desire to study.

Man is created with certain desires beforehand, and nobody knows why he is created that way and why his desires are displayed in a particular way.

Ranking and selection in a group takes place naturally before a permanent group is constituted.

Nobody, except for Haim Vital, understood the Ari properly. The Ari, Rabbi Isaac Luria, lived in the mid 16th century and taught in Safed.

It is known that Haim Vital undertook to study by following the new method worked out by the Ari. There were already great Kabbalists in the group of the Ari, but he nevertheless transmitted everything to Haim Vital exclusively.

The way a master in Kabbalah teaches depends on the type of souls which descend to this world.

Prior to the Ari, there were other systems of teaching, other methods. Following the disclosure of the Ari's methods, it is possible for everybody to study; only a genuine desire is required.

The Baal HaSulam, Rabbi Y. Ashlag, did not modify the system of the Ari, he only extended it. He gave more detailed commentaries on the books of the Ari and the Zohar.

It is in this way that those in our generation who want to study Kabbalah and draw themselves closer to the spiritual realm may understand the inner essence of the studied material, and may establish analogies when reading the Bible (The Five Books of Moses, the Prophets and the Scriptures).

The souls that entered this world prior to the Ari perceived the spiritual as purely extrinsic. After the Ari's death, souls began to descend, and they studied and analyzed themselves and the spiritual world by means of a spiritual and scientific method.

This is the reason why the books issued before the Ari, are written in a narration format.

The books subsequent to the Ari's teaching, e.g. the Study of the Ten Sefirot, are written using the language of *Behinot* (Phases), the *Sefirot* and the *Olamot* (Worlds). It is a psychological engineering, a scientific approach to the soul.

For a great Kabbalist there is no reason to be engaged in the sciences of our world, to carry out different experiments and discoveries.

He may provide all the explanations from the point of view of the Kabbalah, because it is the source of all sciences.

Each science possesses its own language. If the Kabbalist is not a scientist he will not be able to describe different phenomena using the required scientific terminology.

The Kabbalist perceives the true laws of the Universe, which are the foundation of the material and spiritual essence of all things.

In what language might he write the correlation between two objects? And what are the relations between spiritual objects? How can he describe the spiritual force which holds this entire world together?

No specific formula in this world can convey all this. In the spiritual world, the Kabbalist may be able to pass on all his perceptions, though how can these perceptions be made available to the layman?

Even if it were possible to somehow narrate, nothing could be applied to our world until man changes his egoistic nature.

If people could modify their attributes to a higher level, they would be able to communicate amongst themselves in a spiritual language and perform spiritual deeds.

Each person receives and suffers according to the level on which he stands. To rise to a spiritual level, a Screen (*Masach*) is required and this is no easy task.

Man, as it were, is trapped inside a vicious circle from which he cannot escape. He thus ignores what is beyond it.

This is why Kabbalah is called a secret science for those who do not know about its workings.

In his Introduction to the Book of the Zohar the Kabbalist Baal HaSulam talks about the four degrees of knowledge: (i) substance, (ii) form clothed in substance, (iii) abstract form and (iv) essence.

Science may only study substance and substance with a form. Form without substance is a purely abstract conception and does not lend itself to accurate analysis. The last, essence, which is what animates objects and triggers reactions, is unknowable.

The same applies to the spiritual world. Even a great Kabbalist may, while studying something spiritual, perceive substance and its makeup, in whichever form, though never the form without a substance.

Thus, in the spiritual dimension, there is also a limit to our knowledge of the Universe.

Finally, when a Kabbalist reaches a certain required level, he receives a present from Above, and the secrets of the Universe are disclosed to him.

Lesson 9

Topics examined in this lesson:

Lesson 9

The birth of the five worlds:

(i)   *Adam Kadmon*

(ii) *Atzilut*

(iii) *Beria*

(iv) *Yetzira*

(v)   *Assiya*

   is actually the realization of the five *Sefirot*: *Keter*, *Hochma*, *Bina*, *Zeir Anpin*, and *Malchut*, which were in *Malchut* itself.

   The spreading of the worlds from Above to Below matches the progressive increase of the *Aviut* of the four desires or phases from 0 to 4.

   The worlds are like a sphere surrounding *Malchut*. As an analogy, you can picture a man surrounded by spheres and using his organs of sensation to perceive only the sphere that is closest to him: the World of *Assiya*.

   By sharpening his organs of sensation and by modifying his qualities, man begins gradually to perceive the next sphere, and so on.

   All the worlds are a sort of filter placed in the Light's path, a special Screen that blocks the Surrounding Light: the *Ohr Makif*.

   As soon as man senses the presence of these worlds, he removes the "screen-filters." This draws him closer to the Creator.

   If the Light reached man without being filtered, it would bring about the *Shevirat haKelim* of man's Vessels.

By removing all "Screen-Worlds" man allows all the worlds to penetrate him. At this stage man acquires the Light and possesses attributes similar to the Light's.

Such a state of being is associated with *Gmar Tikkun*—the Final Correction.

In the beginning, a man is located inside the worlds and he perceives their power and the constraints imposed upon him.

How can one overcome these constraints? By performing an inner correction, corresponding for instance to the attributes of the World of *Assiya*. This means being an altruist on level zero.

After having been overcome, the World of *Assiya* penetrates man and can be sensed by him.

In order to sense the World of *Yetzira*, it is necessary to acquire attributes similar to those of this world and to allow this world to penetrate us.

At this stage we become level one altruists. The goal is to let all the worlds in, and to become similar to these worlds according to the following degrees of *Aviut*: 2, 3, 4.

By this means, *Malchut* is fully corrected and absorbs the first nine *Sefirot*, while man moves beyond the limits of all the worlds and reaches the World of Infinity (*Olam Ein Sof*).

To begin correction man needs to aspire to the attributes of the Creator as well as attain his own.

Each new *Partzuf* of the World of *Atzilut* starts from the *Peh* of the previous *Partzuf*, except the *Partzufim* of *Zeir Anpin* and *Malchut*; *Zeir Anpin* starts from the *Tabur* of *Abba ve Ima* and *Malchut* starts from the *Tabur* of *Zeir Anpin*.

The three *Partzufim* of *Atik*, *Arich Anpin*, and *Abba ve Ima* are called *Keter*, *Hochma* and *Bina* and this corresponds to *Keter*, *Hochma* and *Bina* of the World of *Nikudim*.

Rosh of the World of *Atzilut* corresponds to the two Heads of the World of *Nikudim* and fulfills the same function. *Rosh* of the World of *Atzilut*, which consist of *Atik*, *Arich Anpin* and *Abba ve Ima*, was the first to emerge on the *Reshimot* of the non-broken *Kelim* of the World of *Nikudim*.

However, *Zeir Anpin* and *Malchut* are gradually restored. Only *Galgalta ve Eynaim* is restored from *Zeir Anpin* and a single point from *Malchut*.

AHPs of *Zeir Anpin* and *Malchut* are in the Worlds of *BYA*. If these *AHPs* are corrected, then all worlds are corrected.

The correction is carried out with the help of the *Partzuf* of *Adam HaRishon*.

What is this *Partzuf* of *Adam HaRishon* like? *Malchut* of the World of *Atzilut* is raised to the level of *Bina*. This is achieved in three phases. The whole World of *Atzilut* then ascends three levels.

The normal condition of the World of *Atzilut* is called "a weekday." During such days the World of *Atzilut* is illuminated by an incomplete Light which spreads down to the *Parsa*.

After this, a greater Light comes down from Above and grants higher attributes to the World of *Atzilut*, making it move up one level.

Now *Malchut* is located in the place of *Zeir Anpin*. *Zeir Anpin* now reaches the level of *Abba ve Ima*. *Abba ve Ima* replace *Arich Anpin*, which in turn rises to the level of *Atik*, which finally rises even higher into *SAG*.

The first elevation of the World of *Atzilut* takes place on Friday evening, *Erev Shabbat*.

Such a progression is called arousal from Above, *itaruta de lema'ala*, in Aramaic. In our world this corresponds to days, weeks, time and all that is not dependent on us but dependent on the laws of nature and over which we have no control.

The next phase elevates the World of *Atzilut* one level higher. *Malchut* now stands on the level of *Abba ve Ima*, where it is endowed with an additional attribute: the intention to give.

At this stage *Malchut* may receive, for the Creator's sake. It now has a Screen and is able to perform a *Zivug de Aka'a*, thus creating new *Partzufim*.

Based on the attributes of *Abba ve Ima* on the one hand, and on the attributes of the *Malchut* of the *Ein Sof*, on the other hand, *Malchut* creates a new *Partzuf: Adam HaRishon*.

For a Kabbalist, spiritual states, called *Erev Shabbat* (Friday evening), *Shabbat* (Saturday), *Motzei Shabbat* (Saturday evening) may be experienced on days bearing no connection to the calendar.

While on the *Shabbat* it is prohibited to smoke or to travel in a vehicle, in the personal *Shabbat*, everything is allowed.

That's because the Kabbalist lives in this world and is compelled to do and obey its laws.

Thus, for a Kabbalist six days may last a split second, while *Shabbat* may last several days. These two kinds of things are totally incomparable.

Everything that occurs in this world relates to our body, but what takes place in the spiritual world relates to the soul.

For the time being, we can witness that our soul and body are not synchronized.

But in the future, when our world will operate with the same principles as the spiritual worlds, which will happen when the *Gmar Tikkun* is achieved, all the deeds of the two worlds as well as all the times will merge together.

If you changed and this has taken you one second, and your next change takes five years, then this means that your next second will have lasted five years.

In the spiritual world time is measured by the transformation of one's attributes. A thousand years may elapse in our world before a man begins to study Kabbalah.

Upon entering the spiritual, we are able to live in a day what we used to live in several lives. This is an example of transformation and shrinking of time.

Spiritual years correspond to the 6,000 degree levels of *BYA* and they cannot be matched with our material time referential.

Ascent from the Worlds of *BYA* to the World of *Atzilut* is called Saturday, Sabbath or *Shabbat*. The portion ranging between *Tabur* of *Galgalta* and the *Parsa* is called *Shabbat*.

The first ascent is the ascent of the World of *Beria* to the World of *Atzilut*, the second one is the ascent of the World of *Yetzira* to the World of *Atzilut*, and the third one relates to the World of *Assiya*.

The ascent of the Worlds of *BYA* and the World of *Atzilut* takes place simultaneously.

When the third phase of ascent occurs, the World of *Atzilut* encompasses the *Zeir Anpin* and the *Malchut* of *Atzilut* and the Worlds of *BYA*.

At this time the *Rosh* of the World of *Atzilut*: *Atik, Arich Anpin, Abba ve Ima*, duly cross the boundaries of the World of *Atzilut* and enter the World of *Adam Kadmon*.

The *Rosh* of *Galgalta* ascends in its turn (Phase 1 of the ascent) together with *Rosh AB* (Phase 2 of the ascent), and with *Rosh SAG* (Phase 3 of the ascent) and enters the World of *Ein Sof.*

A man who reaches the first spiritual World of *Assiya* may, during the third phase of ascent, reach the World of *Atzilut* and experience the spiritual *Shabbat.*

This man would then be brought back to his initial state, because his ascent was not the result of his own efforts, but received as a gift from Above.

The direction of spiritual time is always from the bottom up. All souls, all of mankind, without being aware of the process, are constantly ascending, getting closer to the Creator in order to bond with Him.

This is called the direct flow of spiritual time. Time always is measured in the positive direction even if man may feel the process as being negative.

Man is egoistic, that is why the spiritual is perceived as negative. However, man never degrades himself when he walks the path of spiritual progression.

In this world man should not seek to inflate his egoism, rather he should long to come closer to the Creator instead.

While working in this direction until his final correction, man will increasingly sense his growing egoism, i.e. his natural egoism will be worsened compared to the divine attributes.

The study of Kabbalah implies the attraction of the Surrounding Light (*Ohr Makif*) whose function is to reveal to man what his true attributes are. These appear ever more negative, albeit they have remained unchanged.

In fact, man has only become more aware of the true nature of his attributes under the influence of the Divine Light. This sensation is an indication that man has made progress, even if he believes to the contrary.

What are the Worlds of *BYA* like? They are the altruistic *Kelim* which have fallen into the *AHP* below the *Parsa*. These worlds are also divided into *Galgalta ve Eynaim* and *AHPs*. Their *Galgalta ve Eynaim* ends in the *Chazeh* (Chest) of the World of *Yetzira*, i.e. after the ten *Sefirot* of the World of *Beria* and the six *Sefirot* of the World of *Yetzira*.

The fourteen lower *Sefirot* from the *Chazeh* of *Yetzira* and below (four *Sefirot* of the World of *Yetzira* and ten *Sefirot* of the World of *Assiya*) are the *AHPs* of the Worlds of *BYA*.

The World of *Atzilut* illuminates with its Light the Worlds of *BYA* all the way down to the *Chazeh* of the World of *Yetzira*. The World of *Atzilut* is called *Shabbat*.

The sixteen upper *Sefirot* of the Worlds of *BYA* (*Galgalta ve Eynaim*), from the *Parsa* to the *Chazeh*, are called the "Domain of *Shabbat*" (*Tehum Shabbat*) but the World of *Atzilut* itself is called *Yir* (city).

Even when all the Worlds of *BYA* ascend to the World of *Atzilut*, it is still possible to work with desires located below the *Parsa* up to the *Chazeh* of the World of *Yetzira* (*Galgalta ve Eynaim*).

That is why in our world, it is allowed during *Shabbat* to cross the limits of the city, but only in the limits of the city within the boundaries of *Tehum Shabbat*.

This distance is measured as 2000 *ama* (approximately 3000 feet) and 70 *ama*. How is this distance divided?

From the *Parsa* to the *Chazeh* of the World of *Beria* it is called *Ibur* and equals 70 *ama*. This distance is included in the World of *Atzilut* even though it is located outside it. It is an outer strip surrounding the city. The distance from the *Chazeh* of the world *Beria* to the *Chazeh* of the World of *Yetzira* equals 2000 *ama*.

The whole distance between the *Parsa* and the *Sium* is 6,000 *ama*. The portion of the Worlds of *BYA* stretching from the *Chazeh* of *Yetzira* to the *Sium* is called "a filthy place"— *Mador Klipot* (the place of the Husks).

This *Mador Klipot* is composed of the *AHPs* of the Worlds of *BYA*, which embrace the four *Sefirot* of the World of *Yetzira* and the ten *Sefirot* of the World of *Assiya*. It is a place absolutely devoid of sanctity (*Kedusha*), one cannot go there during *Shabbat*.

In Israel, cities are surrounded by a special wired fence, which indicates that everything within this fence is related to the city. It is called an *Eruv* and it creates a unified territory for this city. Within these limits it is permitted to walk, to bring things in and out.

When a man ascends to the spiritual world and crosses the *Machsom*, he need not go through the *Mador Klipot*. For him the transition to the spiritual does not take place during *Shabbat*, when the Worlds of *BYA* are in the World of *Atzilut*.

The spiritual *Shabbat* does not begin at the same time for everybody.

In our world, *Shabbat* sets in at different times in different countries and cities, but if a man is not under the influence of the sun or the moon, for example in the cosmos, he has to adjust his *Shabbat* with Jerusalem time: in accordance with the spiritual understanding that the Creator is in Jerusalem.

The souls are lifted to the World of *Atzilut* to show them what inherent limits exist there, so that they can keep within them.

When a man sets himself limits he does not notice them, he is above these limitations, and they are not constraining.

Then the actions man undertakes stem from his own attributes. The goal of Creation implies a personal ascent, and *Shabbat* exists in order to show man what exists in the higher worlds, what there is to strive for.

The achievement of correction is when the Light of the Creator shines directly, no longer through the worlds that act like filters.

The shining of the Light is unbounded and brings unbridled delight to fulfill the goal of Creation.

Lesson 10

Topics examined in this lesson:

Lesson 10

To summarize what we have covered so far:

Adam HaRishon is the only created being. This *Partzuf* reaches the height of the three worlds: *Beria*, *Yetzira* and *Assiya*. Its Head is in the World of *Beria*, the *Garon* (Throat) spreads to the *Chazeh* of the World of *Yetzira*, its *Guf* (Body) is from the *Chazeh* of the World of *Yetzira* stretching all the way to the limits of this world. The *Raglaim* (Feet) are on the place of the World of *Assiya*.

How are the countries situated in the worlds?

The Baal HaSulam says the following, using the language of the Branches: the World of *Atzilut* is called *Eretz Yisrael* (the land of Israel). The nearest place to it, Jordan, is on the place of the World of *Beria*.

Upon the Creator's command two tribes of Israel, two parts of the souls may be situated in Jordan, i.e. in the World of *Beria*, as the attributes of this world (attributes of *Bina*) only differ slightly from the attributes of the World of *Atzilut* (*Hochma*).

Syria is considered adjacent to Israel; it is called *Malchut* of the World of *Beria*. Then, from the *Malchut* of the World of *Beria*, up to the *Chazeh* of the World of *Yetzira*, we find the location of Babylon.

It is evident that the distance from the *Parsa* up to the *Chazeh* of the World of *Yetzira* still corresponds to *Eretz Yisrael* and is called *Kibbush David*, David's conquests.

King David materialized the spiritual in our world. Everything that we study about the spiritual must be materialized in this world, at least once.

There are only the Creator and man, i.e. the desire to give delight and the desire to enjoy this delight.

There are five filters around man which conceal the Light of the Creator, five worlds.

If a man acts naturally, according to all his desires, he finds himself under the influence of these filters. All of them are above him.

But if a man decides to correct himself in accordance with the properties of just one of these filters, even the lowest of them, he will ascend. He will stand above the filter and his attributes will match the attributes of the given world.

Furthermore, if his attributes become similar to those of the other two worlds, he will neutralize the action of these two filters as well, and will find himself above them.

Then the Light of the Creator will shine directly through his soul. Everything that happens to us between life and death is a consequence of what takes place in the spiritual worlds.

The Light wants to enter *Malchut* regardless of its condition. Man has to push the Light away even though he can receive it.

We are now experiencing *Tzimtzum*, and it seems to us that the Creator no longer wants us to perceive Him, that is why He conceals Himself.

Actually, if a man, for example, performs a correction equal to the World of *Assiya*, then this means he is located in this world.

He has removed the filter he no longer needs as he can now retain the Light and receive it for the sake of giving. Then he realizes that for the Creator it does not matter whether we are making the restriction in order to receive for His sake or for our own.

Simply, man himself reaches a moral level where there is no distinction between receiving or giving, truth and lies, good deeds and transgressions.

Man himself chooses what he prefers. But on the Creator's side there is only one desire, to delight man. The type of delight depends on the receiver.

The main aspect is, without any conditions set by the Creator, to choose the altruistic ascent even though no additional reward or punishment will be incurred.

This choice is not on the punishment-reward level, but on the highest spiritual level where selflessness and detachment prevail.

The Creator places five filters in front of man, to seal him off from the Divine Light. Behind the last, the fifth filter, the Creator is not sensed at all. This is where our material world is located.

There also, life is supported by a tiny spark of Light (*Ner Dakik*), which is the meaning of our life, the sum of all our desires from all generations, in all souls, since the dawn of mankind.

This Light is so minute that the deeds carried out by the souls are not considered transgressions but are merely considered as minimal animal life.

There is no restriction on receiving these minimal pleasures. Live and enjoy ...

However, if you want more, you have to become similar to the spiritual. Each spiritual pleasure means committing a completely altruistic bestowal regardless of yourself.

To achieve this it is necessary for man to reach a certain level and act like the filter itself, by shielding away the incoming Light with the help of his moral strength.

The filter then ceases to exist for such a man, and he is able to push away the Light that strives to enter his *Kli*. This man will later on receive, but for the sake of the Creator.

The soul of Adam conformed to the 30 *Sefirot* of the three Worlds of *BYA*, which represent the same World of *Atzilut*, but are located inside egoistic desires with an *Aviut Bet*, *Aviut Gimel* and *Aviut Dalet*.

When Adam corrects his actions, spiritualizes them, he ascends together with the worlds to the World of *Atzilut*.

After passing through the 6,000 degrees of correction, *Adam HaRishon* fully ascends to the World of *Atzilut*.

Each soul, being a fragment of the *Partzuf* of *Adam HaRishon*, follows the same path.

Man himself cannot choose what needs to be corrected, but corrects what is sent to him from Above, what is revealed to him. And so on till the highest level.

Index to the Ten Kabbalah Lessons

Other Books by
Rabbi Michael Laitman

An Interview With The Future

"Kabbalah is not about researching an ancient mystical body of knowledge, but is rather the most modern science that is closest to man. It is the science of the 21st century that researches the forces that we do not see, forces that govern our world and influence every moment of our lives. This is a science that will change the future of each and every individual, and all of mankind. The sources explain very clearly that once this process is underway, the entire world will gradually elevate itself to a higher state of being."

Rabbi Michael Laitman

According to Rabbi Laitman, ours is the first generation on earth with the ability to draw the future closer so that we can experience our time here in a much more pleasant manner. But what is hard for us to grasp is that that we do not necessarily need to know what the future holds in order to reach that state. And in our current state, we do not even have the ability to comprehend what that future form will feel like.

So we can either continue to advance as we have been doing since the beginning of time, or use this infinite source of knowledge to control our destiny. We can actively embrace this ultimate source of fulfillment to reduce suffering in the world, or continue to wait and see what happens next.

Since a Kabbalist is a person who has attained the spiritual realm, they are completely aware of the processes influencing our world. *An Interview With The Future* by the Israel based Kabbalist Michael Laitman, is the defining book of the decade. It is a meeting with destiny that provides the key to safeguarding the future of the entire human race.

The Kabbalah Experience

The wisdom of Kabbalah teaches us how to live in the reality that is spread before us. It is a systematic method that has evolved over thousands of years through a handful of unique individuals in every generation. During all that time it was concealed from the public eye that was not yet ready to receive it, until the current generation—the generation, for which this method was specifically developed. That is why it is written in the Zohar, that from 1995 onward Kabbalah will become a way of life, open to all with no restrictions.

Why our generation? Because the souls that descend to this world and dress in our bodies evolve from generation to generation, until they come to a state where a question awakens in them about the meaning of their very existence. If we contemplate reality as it is described in the books of Kabbalists who speak of 'the end of days'— which we are at the threshold of—there arises a profound fear that without Kabbalah, we will not be able to secure the safe passage to the higher level of being that awaits us.

Kabbalah allows us to come to know the spiritual world—the very system that monitors and leads reality, including the reality of this world, the whole of humanity and each and every one of us at any given moment. Through this method, we can control the system of the worlds and determine how to conduct our daily lives.

Attaining the Worlds Beyond

Attaining the Worlds Beyond is a first step toward discovering the ultimate fulfillment of spiritual ascent in our lifetime. This book reaches out to all those who are searching for answers, who are seeking a logical and reliable way to understand the world's phenomena.

This magnificent introduction to the wisdom of Kabbalah provides a new kind of awareness that enlightens the mind, invigorates the heart, and moves the reader to the depths of their soul. the Worlds Beyond is a first step toward discovering the ultimate fulfillment of spiritual ascent in our lifetime. This book reaches out to all those who are searching for answers, who are seeking a logical and reliable way to understand the world's phenomena. This magnificent introduction to the wisdom of Kabbalah provides a new kind of awareness that enlightens the mind, invigorates the heart, and moves the reader to the depths of their soul.

World Center For Kabbalah Studies

WWW.KABBALAH.INFO

The Largest Source of Free Spiritual Content in the World

Participate in Live Zohar Lessons

Access Free e-Books

Listen to Kabbalah Music

Join lively discussions

Download the latest lessons

Enjoy Kabbalah material
in over 20 languages!

Make friends around the world

www.kabbalah.info